TRADE
REFORM

THE INTERNATIONAL CENTER FOR ECONOMIC GROWTH is a nonprofit research institute founded in 1985 to stimulate international discussions on economic policy, economic growth, and human development. The Center sponsors research, publications, and conferences in cooperation with an international network of correspondent institutes, which distribute publications of both the Center and other network members to policy audiences around the world. The Center's research and publications program is organized around five series: Sector Studies; Country Studies; Studies in Human Development and Social Welfare; Occasional Papers; and Reprints.

The Center is affiliated with the Institute for Contemporary Studies, and has headquarters in Panama and a home office in San Francisco, California.

For further information, please contact the International Center for Economic Growth, 243 Kearny Street, San Francisco, California, 94108, USA. Phone (415) 981-5353; Fax (415) 986-4878.

ICEG Board of Overseers

TRADE REFORM

Lessons from Eight Countries

Edited by
Geoffrey Shepherd
and
Carlos Geraldo Langoni

An International Center for Economic Growth Publication

ICS PRESS
San Francisco, California

Inquiries, book orders, and catalog requests should be addressed to ICS Press, 243 Kearny Street, San Francisco, California, 94108. Telephone: (415) 981-5353; FAX: (415) 986-4878.

Index compiled by Shirley Kessel.

Cover designed by John Paul, JPD Communications & Design.

Distributed to the trade by National Book Network, Lanham, Maryland.

Library of Congress Cataloging-in-Publication Data

Trade reform: lessons from eight countries/edited by Geoffrey Shepherd and Carlos Geraldo Langoni.
    p.   cm.
    "An International Center for Economic Growth Publication."
    Includes bibliographical references and index.
    ISBN 1-55815-097-8. — ISBN 1-55815-086-2 (pbk.)
    1. Commercial policy—Case studies. 2. International economic relations. 3. Latin America—Commercial policy—Case studies. 4. Europe—Commercial policy—Case studies. 5. East Asia—Commercial policy—Case studies. I. Shepherd, Geoffrey, 1943–   II. Langoni, Carlos Geraldo.

HF1411.T7134 1991   90-45771
382′ .3—dc20   CIP

Contents

List of Tables

List of Figures

Preface

Throughout the developing world countries are abandoning systems of extensive protection and are opening up to foreign trade, as they recognize that restrictive trade policies have been costly to their economies, underwriting inefficiency and limiting growth. The question asked is not whether restrictive trade regimes should be reformed but what measures should be taken, how rapidly, and in what sequence to achieve trade reform without excessive transition costs.

Analyzing the experience of eight countries that have attempted trade reform during the past four decades, the authors of this book find a number of lessons for successful liberalization. One recurrent theme is the importance of monetary and fiscal policy. Radical reform of the foreign-exchange regime, undergirded by policies of economic stabilization, has initiated every significant and lasting trade liberalization.

Some surprising lessons emerge from the country studies: Although adjustment costs—in particular, possible unemployment—are to be expected in the transition from restricted to freer trade, there is little evidence to suggest that the liberalization episodes studied have led to net unemployment, even in the manufacturing sector. Moreover, major initial relaxation of quantitative restrictions on imports—a key step in sustaining reform attempts—appears typically to have been achieved with few transitory costs and with a major increase in economic growth.

This book grew out of a conference held in 1988 in São Paulo, Brazil, to consider some of the results of a massive World Bank research project on implementing trade reform. The conclusions of this project are powerful and will have a forceful impact on a world economy already inclined to seek the benefits of open trade. The International Center for

Economic Growth is pleased to publish this volume, in which the lessons of liberalization experience are made accessible to anyone who wants to understand the relation between policy and outcome in trade reform.

Nicolás Ardito-Barletta
General Director
International Center for Economic Growth

Panama City, Panama
January 1991

Editors' Preface

This volume is based on the papers presented at a conference entitled "Por uma Nova Política de Comércio Exterior do Brasil" (Toward a New Trade Policy for Brazil). The conference was held at the Maksoud Plaza Hotel, São Paulo, Brazil, on April 11 and 12, 1988. It was jointly organized by the Center for World Economy, of the Fundação Getúlio Vargas (Rio de Janeiro), and the World Bank (Washington, D.C.).

We are grateful for the contributions made to the conference by those acting as discussants, chairmen, and roundtable participants:

- Mário Amato, president, Federação das Indústrias do Estado de São Paulo

- Renato Baumann das Neves, external-sector coordinator, IPLAN/Instituto de Planejamento, Brasília

- Alfredo Baumgarten, Fundação Getúlio Vargas, Rio de Janeiro

- Luiz Gonzaga Belluzo, Fundação de Apoio a Pesquisa do Estado de São Paulo

- Carlos Alberto Primo Braga, professor, Fundação Instituto de Pesquisas Econômicas, Universidade de São Paulo

- Helson Braga, Instituto de Planejamento Econômico e Social, Rio de Janeiro

- Luiz Carlos Bresser Pereira, director, Cia. Pão de Atúcar, São Paulo, and professor, Fundação Getúlio Vargas.

- José L. Carvalho, professor, Universidade Santa Ursula, Rio de Janeiro

- Armeane M. Choksi, director, Brazil Department, the World Bank, Washington, D.C.

- Roberto Gianetti da Fonseca, vice president, Cotia Finance Co. Ltd., São Paulo

- Samuel Pinheiro Guimarães, chief of the Economics Department, Ministry of External Relations, Brasília

- Roberto d'Utra Vaz, vice president, Cia. IOCHPE de Participações, São Paulo

- Norberto Ingo Zadrozny, president, Associação de Comércio Exterior do Brasil, Rio de Janeiro

We owe an important debt to our colleague, Antonio Pimenta-Neves, of the World Bank, who did much to set up and organize the conference.

We would also like to acknowledge the support provided by the *Gazeta Mercantil*, the leading Brazilian business newspaper, in publicizing the conference.

The findings, interpretations, and conclusions expressed in this book are entirely those of the authors and should not be attributed in any manner to the World Bank, to its affiliated organizations, or to members of its Board of Executive Directors or the countries they represent.

Geoffrey Shepherd
Carlos Geraldo Langoni

Washington, D.C.
Rio de Janeiro
January 1991

GEOFFREY SHEPHERD AND
CARLOS GERALDO LANGONI

CHAPTER ONE

Introduction

The superiority of free trade has been demonstrated by numerous empirical studies and has become increasingly accepted by policy makers in developing countries.[1] The problem of transition from a restrictive regime to one of liberalized trade, however, has not been studied extensively; and little is known about the essential attributes of a successful policy path, particularly about issues of timing and sequencing in the reform of trade policy. These issues were the focus of a research project whose conclusions are outlined in this book.

All but one of the chapters in this volume summarize some of the findings of the project, "The Timing and Sequencing of a Trade Liberalization Policy," conducted by the World Bank from 1984 to 1988 and drawing on the experience of past trade-reform efforts in developing countries as a source of lessons about how countries might best go about designing the trade-reform process. The creators of the project had in mind two meanings of freer trade (or trade liberalization) as the objective toward which reform was aimed: first, a reduction in the levels and dispersion of rates of protection; second, a change in the form of protection from quantitative restrictions to tariffs. These two elements often appear together, but occasionally they may be in conflict.

The Research Project

The questions posed by the project were: What are the characteristics of successful and unsuccessful trade liberalization attempts; and how, according to past experience, can trade liberalization best be implemented? The project identified several major issues, to some extent interrelated, as playing an important role in determining the fate of any attempted liberalization:

- What is the appropriate speed and intensity of liberalization?

- Is it desirable to have a separate policy stage of replacing nonprice forms of trade restrictions with price measures?

- Is it desirable to treat productive activities uniformly, during the process of trade liberalization, or differentially?

- If a uniform treatment is indicated, how should it be formulated?

- On what pattern of the economy's performance is the fate of a liberalization policy likely to hinge?

- Is it desirable to have a stage of export promotion? If so, what should be its timing in relationship to import liberalization?

- What are the appropriate circumstances for the introduction of a liberalization policy?

- How important are exogenous developments in determining the likelihood that liberalization will be sustainable?

- Finally, what other policy measures are important, in either their presence or their absence, for a successful policy of trade liberalization?

Looming behind many of these issues are the potential adjustment costs of a liberalization policy and, in particular, the possible impact of trade liberalization on the unemployment of labor. The World Bank study also explicitly addressed this crucial issue.

The research project investigated the experience of liberalization in the postwar world and covered almost all episodes that could be found in developing countries. These experiences were analyzed in nineteen country studies, covering thirty-seven separate liberalization episodes, following a common pattern of inquiry. The project has yielded inferences not only at the level of the individual studies but also in a synthesis study that compared the patterns observed in the thirty-seven liberalization episodes. The complete study is being published in seven volumes.[2]

The São Paulo Conference

During the same period when the World Bank was about to conclude this large, cross-country research project, a conference titled "Toward a New Trade Policy for Brazil" was held in São Paulo on April 11 and 12, 1988. The conference attracted some 400 participants from government, business, and universities.

The Brazilian context for the conference was shaped by developments in Brazilian trade policy in the 1980s. Postwar Brazil, like many other developing countries, has made use of high levels of protection (among other policies) to attract resources into the production of manufactures for the domestic market. Following the onset of the debt crisis in 1982, the Brazilian economy was forced into a process of deflation and imposition of draconian import controls to balance the external account. The policy has been to use the discretionary rationing of foreign exchange and through import licensing to provide absolute protection to virtually all local industrial production. The trade policy has been costly to the economy: it has underwritten inefficiency, uncertainties have grown, and the deadweight costs of doing business in a primarily bureaucratically controlled system have increased.

The presentation of the international evidence on trade-policy reforms stimulated a substantial debate among the Brazilian conference participants about trade reform in their own country. What emerged was a strong consensus of dissatisfaction with Brazil's existing trade system, only a partial consensus on the general direction of reforms needed, and few visions of how to begin reforms. There was virtually no one to defend the existing system. The bureaucratic nature of controls and the general discontinuity of policies were criticized. The strategy of widespread protection in the name of nurturing infant industries was thought to have run its course.

Ambassador Paulo Tarso Flecha de Lima, then secretary-general of the Ministry of External Relations (Itamaraty), summed up the critical feeling of the conference: "There is no more place for economic autarkies. The last to exist are opening up to foreign trade, and so too should Brazil." Virtually everyone could agree that fewer restrictions on imports and exports were needed for a more open and competitive economy capable of keeping up in the technology race. Similarly, there was consensus that Brazilian trade reform should proceed gradually (even if "gradually" remained undefined). But consensus was absent on some of the key approaches to reform.

First, some participants emphasized the need for a liberalization of the system of allocating foreign exchange as a primary step in the reform process (though they did not agree on what form the liberalization should take). Some others saw such a reform as premature because the Brazilian currency was "weak." Second, views differed on how much domestic reform should be subject to the bargaining process in the Uruguay Round of GATT (General Agreement on Tariffs and Trade). Third, there was no agreement on how trade reform was linked to the external debt problem: some participants saw progress in solving the debt problem as a precondition of trade reform.

With only limited agreement on the nature of reforms needed, it is not surprising that little concrete vision of a reform process was evident. It is clear, however, that to start with, Brazil will have to eliminate non-tariff barriers and will have to unify and simplify tariffs, immediately abolishing all tariff concessions.[3] These changes can then be followed by a process of gradual tariff reduction. The exchange-rate issue will need careful analysis, and the opportunity should be taken to use this instrument of the market to replace the dictates of bureaucracy. A freer system, eventually leading to a floating exchange rate, must be envisaged. A shift toward trade liberalization—adopted not to please Brazil's trading partners but to benefit Brazil itself—will require as a counterpart less protection from Brazil's creditor countries. It must be stressed that trade reform without broader economic reform will lead nowhere: the failure of earlier experiments was due largely to the maintenance of an unsustainable public deficit and to the excessive presence of the state in the economy.

Trade Reform Lessons

Chapter 2 in this volume is based on one of several Brazilian presentations at a roundtable that concluded the São Paulo conference and provides a Brazilian government view of trade reform. The chapter is a particularly important statement of that government's intentions for trade reform and its relationship to the Uruguay Round. The author, Paulo Tarso Flecha de Lima, underlines the inefficiency generated by the present system of protection and the need for a system based on a rationalized tariff structure. (Brazil's major tariff reform occurred a few months after the conference.) Although he envisages a gradualist approach to trade reform, he also takes the position that trade reform is too urgent a need to be postponed in the interest of bargaining within the Uruguay Round.

Chapters 3–10 provide summaries for eight of the nineteen countries in the World Bank study, as well as the major conclusions that have emerged from the overall research project. The eight countries represent a range of successful and unsuccessful trade reform, country characteristics (size, for instance), and approaches to reform (fast or slow, for example).

In Chapter 3, Donald Coes concentrates on the 1964–1973 episode of export-oriented trade reform in Brazil, concluding that it had its success and its failure. The success was a significant positive impact on manufacturing industry without evident employment losses. The failure was, on the one hand, that import liberalization was limited and left in place the bureaucratic control mechanisms that are proving costly to Brazil today and, on the other hand, that exchange-rate policy was not coordinated with policy toward foreign indebtedness. Coes concludes that, since there is evidence that Brazilian exports respond strongly to an improved exchange rate, the country would profit from a greater reliance on exchange-rate policy and a lesser reliance on administrative controls.

Domingo F. Cavallo, in Chapter 4, analyzes Argentina's failed trade-reform experiment in the period 1976–1982. Part of a broader program of economic adjustment, the trade reform was abandoned in 1981 and 1982 during a severe balance-of-payments crisis. Among the reasons for the overvalued real exchange rate that ended the trade reform were the heavy foreign borrowing of the public sector in the late 1970s and the use of an appreciating real exchange rate from 1979 onward as an anti-inflationary device. Among the lessons the author draws is that stronger fiscal control would have been the appropriate anti-inflationary policy, whereas the capital account should have been opened up only after inflation had been brought under control.

Chile's trade reform, as Dominique Hachette describes it in Chapter 5, was undertaken from 1974 to 1979, as part of a broad and ambitious economic reform to reduce inflation and deregulate the economy. By the standards of other episodes studied in the research project the Chilean reform was very rapid. It was also sustained in the difficult conditions of the early 1980s in spite of real exchange-rate appreciation from 1979 (as in Argentina) that resulted from foreign borrowing and the use of the exchange rate in the fight against inflation. The government's ability to resist domestic pressures to reverse the reforms appeared to reflect its political commitment as well as the very success of the past reforms in changing the structure of the economy. Indeed, Chilean imports and exports grew considerably faster than GDP, and the overall employment impact of the reforms was positive (though negative for the manufacturing sector in isolation). Among the lessons of Chilean liberalization Hachette emphasizes the importance of economic stabilization as a prior condition for trade reform and the importance of accompanying reforms in financial and labor markets; the importance, in sequencing trade reforms, of providing transparency in the import regime (by unifying exchange rates and reducing quantitative restrictions) before embarking on tariff reduction; and the importance of providing a favorable and stable regime for exporters in order to build up the political support to sustain the reforms.

In Chapter 6, Demetris Papageorgiou describes Greece's unilateral and bold overnight trade reform of 1953, which started the process of sustained and successful postwar trade liberalization that eventually brought about Greek membership in the European Community. A large devaluation and sudden—and virtually complete—dismantling of a complex and discretionary system of multiple exchange rates and quantitative restrictions was the government's response to the crisis caused by the withdrawal of U.S. aid. The reform initiated an era of exceptional growth in output, real incomes, and profits and of fiscal, price, and external stability. This reform could not have been sustained, however, without the cautious fiscal and monetary policies that characterized the 1950s.

In Chapter 7, Guillermo de la Dehesa reviews four specific reform episodes in the long-term, and largely sustained, opening up of Spain's economy since 1959. The process started with economic stabilization, unification of the exchange rate, partial liberalization of quantitative restrictions, increased incentives to foreign investors, and a rise in import duties. Subsequent reforms, involving further tariff cuts and removal of quantitative restrictions, culminated in Spanish accession to the European Community in 1986, a step that made the reform process irreversible. Reform has helped bring steady growth and disinflation to the economy. Dehesa observes that Spanish trade reform has invariably been initiated when the balance of payments was healthy, but only because trade reform had been preceded by an economic stabilization, itself a response to a crisis such as an external deficit.

In Chapter 8, Oli Havrylyshyn discusses the experience of trade reform in Yugoslavia, where trade policy has emphasized capital-intensive exports. A socialist country with a large debt problem and a large, inefficient state-owned enterprise sector, Yugoslavia attempted in the mid-1960s a mild trade reform emphasizing a discretionary set of export-promotion measures. These measures were reversed at the beginning of the 1970s as the result of overly restrictive macroeconomic policies and inadequate devaluation in the 1960s. Havrylyshyn emphasizes two lessons of the Yugoslav experience. First, selective export promotion, which led to capital-intensive exports not within Yugoslavia's comparative advantage, proved costly. Second, the federal government's political inability to curtail financial assistance to state-owned enterprises impeded the process of adjustment—that is, the process of penalizing inefficiency—that should occur in the wake of a trade reform.

Chapter 9, Richard H. Snape's chapter on East Asia, synthesizes results of two studies, on Korea and Singapore. The author describes three phases of Korean trade reform: a first phase from the early 1960s when export-promotion measures accompanied devaluation; a second phase from 1973 when export incentives were reduced, but selective promotion of heavy- and chemical-industry investments was initiated; and a third phase from 1979 when Korea reverted to more neutral (that is, less selective) policies. Noting that these evolving policies have led to considerable increases in the ratio of both imports and exports to GDP, Snape emphasizes the major policy elements in the successful growth of the trade sector: aggregate incentives to exporting and import-substituting activities that are not significantly different in their average size; relatively little discrimination in the incentives offered to different export activities; the strong commitment of Korean society to competitiveness on world markets; fiscal rectitude; realistic and stable real exchange rates (slowness in liberalizing the capital account contributed to this stability); and flexible policy reactions to internal and external shocks.

Singapore, after a brief and limited flirtation with import substitution (in an economic union with Malaysia in the early 1960s), proceeded to dismantle its interventions in the trade sector and achieved virtually free trade by 1973. Foreign investment has been encouraged, financial markets have been liberalized, and the government has been fiscally conservative. Even though the government has intervened substantially to influence investment decisions, the openness of the economy has, as in Korea, continually subjected this intervention to the test of the market.

Michael Michaely's overview in Chapter 10 is a first attempt to generalize (with all due caution) about the patterns observable in the thirty-seven liberalization episodes studied in the World Bank project. Michaely makes several major observations. First, he finds the following country-specific tendencies: small, resource-poor countries are more likely to liberalize, as too are the more developed of the developing countries. Second, liberalization efforts that begin with strong measures are more likely to survive than those that begin weakly, especially where the historical trade regime was considerably restricted or where past attempts to liberalize have failed. Third, reforms undertaken in a crisis situation are more likely to survive. Fourth—a somewhat unexpected finding—there is little evidence to suggest that the liberalizations studied have led to net unemployment, even in the manufacturing sector. Fifth, the initial level of international reserves does not appear to have been a determining factor in the survival of a liberalization attempt, though trends in exports and reserves were important in explaining the ability of the attempt subsequently to survive. Sixth, a major initial relaxation of quantitative restrictions (rather than tariffs) is a key step in sustaining

most successful liberalization attempts; moreover—again, unexpect-
edly—this step appears typically to have been achieved with few transitory costs and a major increase in economic growth. Finally, the
successful introduction and survival of trade reform are closely linked
to the behavior of the real exchange rate. Depreciations are associated
with success and appreciations with failure; in turn, nominal devaluations accompanied by tight fiscal and monetary policies are almost invariably the policy actions required for real depreciations.

A recurrent theme of the trade-reform case studies presented at the
São Paulo conference, and of the broader research project, relates to the
issues of exchange-rate and macroeconomic reform raised in the preceding paragraph. Reform of the foreign-exchange regime—unification of
exchange rates, devaluation, and abolition of exchange controls—has
initiated every important and sustained trade liberalization. Such a reform could begin only in the wake of fiscal and monetary policies to
reduce the budget deficit and reduce inflation, and it could be sustained
only with the continuation of prudent fiscal and monetary policies. Reform in the foreign-exchange regime needs to be fast; such reform has—
surprisingly, perhaps—provided virtually immediate production gains.
Gradualness is not really an option in reforming the foreign-exchange
regime, but it is an option for reform of residual nontariff barriers and
of tariffs. The lessons of experience suggest that radical reforms in the
foreign-exchange regime, underpinned by policies of economic stabilization, are inescapable realities for countries that wish to tread the path
of trade reform, however gradually.

Notes

1. Studies that demonstrate the superiority of free trade include several major,
multicountry studies, summarized in: Jagdish Bhagwati, *Anatomy and Consequences of Exchange Control Regimes* (Cambridge, Mass.: Ballinger, 1978); Juergen
B. Donges, "A Comparative Study of Industrialization Policies in Fifteen Semi-
Industrialized Countries," *Weltwirtschaftliches Archiv* 112, no. 4, 1976; Anne O.
Krueger, *Liberalization Attempts and Consequences* (Cambridge, Mass.: Ballinger,
1978); and Ian M. D. Little, Tibor Scitovsky, and Maurice F. Scott, *Industry and
Trade in Some Developing Countries: A Comparative Study* (New York: Oxford Uni-
versity Press, 1970).

2. The nineteen country studies are classified by three regions: Latin America
(Argentina, Brazil, Chile, Colombia, Peru, Uruguay), Asia and Pacific (Indone-
sia, Korea, New Zealand, Pakistan, Philippines, Singapore, Sri Lanka), and
Mediterranean (Greece, Israel, Portugal, Spain, Turkey, Yugoslavia).

The overall results of the project, "The Timing and Sequencing of a Trade
Liberalization Policy" (World Bank Research Project 673–31), are contained in

Michael Michaely, Demetris Papageorgiou, and Armeane M. Choksi, *Lessons of Experience in the Developing World*, Liberalizing Foreign Trade, vol. 7 (Oxford: Basil Blackwell, 1990).

Seventeen country studies are contained in vols. 1–6 in the same series, Liberalizing Foreign Trade, edited by Demetris Papageorgiou, Michael Michaely, and Armeane M. Choksi (Oxford: Basil Blackwell, 1990). The contents are as follows:

Vol. 1, *The Experience of Argentina, Chile, and Uruguay*: Domingo Cavallo and Joaquín Cottani, "Argentina"; Sergio de la Cuadra and Dominique Hachette, "Chile"; Edgardo Favaro and Pablo T. Spiller, "Uruguay."

Vol. 2, *The Experience of Korea, the Philippines, and Singapore*: Kwang Suk Kim, "Korea"; Geoffrey Shepherd and Florian Alburo, "The Philippines"; Bee-Yan Aw, "Singapore."

Vol. 3, *The Experience of Israel and Yugoslavia*: Nadav Halevi and Joseph Baruh, "Israel"; Oli Havrylyshyn, "Yugoslavia."

Vol. 4, *The Experience of Brazil, Colombia, and Peru*: Donald V. Coes, "Brazil"; Jorge García García, "Colombia"; Julio J. Nogués, "Peru."

Vol. 5, *The Experience of Indonesia, Pakistan, and Sri Lanka*: Mark M. Pitt, "Indonesia"; Stephen Guisinger and Gerald Scully, "Pakistan"; Andrew G. Cuthbertson and Premachandra Athukorala, "Sri Lanka."

Vol. 6, *The Experience of New Zealand, Spain, and Turkey*: Anthony C. Rayner and Ralph Lattimore, "New Zealand"; Guillermo de la Dehesa, José Juan Ruiz, and Angel Torres, "Spain"; Charles Blitzer and Tercan Baysan, "Turkey."

The study of Portugal is not separately published but is summarized in vol. 7. A further country study has appeared as George C. Kottis, *Liberalizing Foreign Trade: The Experience of Greece*, World Bank Comparative Studies (Washington, D.C.: World Bank, 1989).

3. These remarks and those in the rest of the paragraph represent the gist of some comments made by Carlos Langoni in the course of the conference.

The Multilateral Trade Negotiations and Brazilian Trade-Policy Reform

Central to the April 1988 São Paulo conference on trade reform was an emphasis on the advantages of a liberal import policy. The theoretical arguments for such a policy are well known, but it is the guidance of experience that countries require as they undertake trade reform. Practical cases from Europe, East Asia, and Latin America were presented at the conference. Among these was the case of Brazil itself, which will be discussed in this chapter. In examining the special features of Brazil's experience we need to take into consideration certain facts concerning the Brazilian economy's current place in world trade.

One of the most important factors is the ongoing Uruguay Round of multilateral trade negotiations in Geneva. I have personally participated in this process, meeting regularly with the foreign-trade ministers of the twenty or thirty major developed and developing countries; and I have seen that the interests of Brazil today encompass all the areas under negotiation. There are fifteen working groups in Geneva. Brazil is taking part in all of them, with concrete interests to defend. This involvement is unique among the developing countries. Indeed, few developed countries, beyond the United States, the European Community, and Japan, have such a comprehensive range of interests. Brazil takes part in these negotiations much more as a country of continental dimension, as the world's eighth-largest economy, than as just another member of the heterogeneous group of developing countries. Obviously, though, Brazil does not belong to the other category, that of developed countries. It is to avoid that dichotomy that I evoke the continental dimension of the Brazilian economic system. The special position of Brazil in the world economy means that the country must be prepared to negotiate effectively—that is, if it wishes to obtain real advantages that respond to concrete and specific national interests. Force of circumstance compels Brazil to discard past attitudes, such as those adopted during the Tokyo Round (1973–1979). In those talks Brazil assumed a defensive position, in which it was zealous to secure unilateral treatment in favor of the developing countries and to profit passively from application of the the most-favored-nation clause negotiated among the developed countries but offered practically nothing itself. This rigid attitude was inevitably accompanied by a very limited capacity to influence the normative negotiations on general questions such as subsidies and dumping.

In an exercise like the Uruguay Round, negotiating means deregulating—in other words, one country barters its deregulation measures for other countries' deregulation measures that it deems beneficial. It is for each country to choose what, with whom, and how it will negotiate. This fact should resolve the question of principle concerning the legitimacy of negotiation, a question that seems to have plagued Brazil for so many years. An added argument in favor of active participation by Brazil is that the cycle of development aid that marked the first thirty postwar years, from 1950 to 1980, has clearly run its course. That is an established fact. I have no doubt that the world would be much better if a fruitful dialogue persisted between North and South and if there were effective and disinterested aid to the developing countries. But that era is gone, and we must accept reality.

A negotiating and deregulating Brazilian trade posture must be guided by the following parameters:

- The starting point can only be acceptance by Brazil that its current tariff levels are unrealistic and give rise to a highly distorted import-control system in which prohibitive quotas are combined with frequent exemptions and subjective decisions, all directed by an unnecessary bureaucratic apparatus.

- The next step is therefore to try to restore the basic functions of the customs tariff, which is to serve as the instrument par excellence of import selection, and thereby to promote increasing economic efficiency of the domestic productive system by exposing it to international competition. In other words, a good tariff must simultaneously exercise the necessary measure of control and promote the necessary measure of competition. Brazil's present tariff does neither.

- Another important consideration is that, just as deregulation generates its own dynamism, so excessive protection creates its own inertia. Brazil must not forget that years and years of excessive protection have led to performance levels far short of our intrinsic potential among the most diverse economic agents. Brazilian deregulation, therefore, must not accept the present situation as a basis for mistakenly setting so-called realistic tariff levels. Deregulation must, from the start, promote higher levels of economic productivity through the gradual, progressive, and phased application of new, updated tariff levels. Brazil can set an initial tariff level x and establish a program to arrive at a given level y in a space of, say, four years.

- Finally, any Brazilian deregulation program must take due account of the importance of the country's commitments in ALADI (Latin American Integration Association) and, more particularly, in the accelerating process of integration between Brazil, Argentina, and Uruguay. Favoring those commitments should create no major problems; when adequate tariff levels have been set for third countries it will always be possible to use those levels as guides to grant preference margins, even substantial ones, to Latin American partners.

The positions I have stated are likely to evoke certain negative responses, but I believe there is an effective counterargument for each of these concerns.

First, the process of trade deregulation that I see for Brazil will not cause balance-of-payments difficulties, even temporary ones. Since its primary purpose is to achieve tariff realism, deregulation will not significantly boost imports but will progressively raise the level of domestic economic efficiency. Exports, not imports, will increase, as a consequence of better economic performance.

Next, the argument that, since it is involved in ongoing negotiations in Geneva, Brazil should preserve its bargaining power and negotiate tariff reductions case by case is fallacious. Brazil cannot wait for the progress of the Uruguay Round to determine when it will apply salutary measures to improve its economic efficiency. Moreover, once appropriate tariff levels have been defined for Brazil, the government can negotiate their consolidation in GATT through insertion of the corresponding headings in the Brazilian list. The country will not, therefore, be negotiating additional reductions. Let it not be thought that it would rank as negotiation to present the deregulation of Brazil's external trade as a unilateral gesture of goodwill, to be understood and rewarded by other countries. Trade negotiations do not live by goodwill gestures. A realistic tariff neither increases nor decreases a country's capacity to negotiate tariffs in GATT; the important thing is willingness to negotiate. Consolidating a 30 percent tariff for a particular commodity in GATT has the same commercial significance for a trading partner of Brazil whether the tariff already reflects a realistic estimate or results from a "shrewd" negotiation from the prohibitive level of 150 percent to the real one of 30 percent.

Finally, there is the argument that if domestic saving and investment capacity are low it is not the time to expose the Brazilian economic system to higher levels of competition and the modernization efforts that this competition would entail. The argument is attractive, because it is linked to the idea that improving economic performance always calls for new injections of capital. It bears repeating, however, that excessive protection for an unjustifiably long period has generated low levels of domestic productivity that are also unjustified. We can therefore assume that Brazil today possesses a reasonable margin for adaptation to external competition. There is productive capacity ready to be harnessed through better resource management, better manpower utilization, and higher and more modern levels of administrative efficiency—without fresh injections of capital and therefore without sacrificing scarce domestic savings. We could even expect that in improving the sectoral and overall efficiency of its economic system Brazil would correspondingly boost its domestic savings rate and thereby equip itself to invest more and invest better.

Brazil: Precedents and Prospects in Foreign Trade

Shortly after the change of political regime in 1964, Brazil initiated a series of reforms in its foreign-trade policy. During the years that followed, the economy was increasingly opened to foreign trade, both through eased restrictions on imports and through export incentives. This trend continued until 1974, when it was interrupted by the first oil shock. In the following decade, Brazil reverted to a much more restrictive policy on imports, while exports lost the momentum they had gained in previous years.[1] In spite of various efforts to relieve the pressures on the external accounts and to increase the capacity to import, Brazil's economy is today more protected from foreign trade than it was fifteen years ago.

Brazil's experiment in foreign-trade policy during the period 1965–1973 is examined in a larger work that is a result of the comparative project undertaken by the World Bank (Coes 1990). This chapter uses Brazil's experience in the years before the oil shock as the starting point for a discussion of its current problems and prospects in foreign trade policy. The first section is a summary of the events explored in the World Bank study. The next section presents an analysis of the principal conclusions that can validly be drawn from the Brazilian experience; and the third section goes on to deal with the present situation, concluding with a discussion of the relevance of the earlier period to Brazil's current foreign-trade policy.

Reforms between 1964 and 1974

The immediate concern of the government that took power in 1964 was not foreign trade but controlling inflation, which, although low by the standards of the 1980s, was at levels unprecedented in 1964. In external economic policy the priority objectives of the new administration were a resumption of capital flows to Brazil and access to the international market.

Policy measures directed toward foreign trade were soon implemented, however. An important feature of the process that opened Brazil to world markets between 1964 and 1974 was the emphasis given to exports—not just to the removal of restrictions on imports, as in liberalization of a purely orthodox and conventional kind. The initial policy measures sought to reduce the implicit discrimination in Brazil's tax structure, which made its products, especially manufactured products using imported materials subject to various Brazilian taxes, more expensive than others on the international market. In November 1964, Law 4502 exempted imports from the Tax on Industrial Products (IPI). A second incentive was a reduction in the tax on company earnings as a function of the share of output exported. A third measure, which had already existed in a formal sense since 1957, was the reformulation and implementation of "drawback," which exempted from taxation imports destined for use in export products. Reforms in import policy came later, only after an improvement in Brazil's current account as a result of the 1965–1966 stabilization program and a decline in economic growth. Import reform was introduced in March 1967, when many tariffs were reduced to less than half their previous levels.

The new tariff structure was soon followed by an important change in macroeconomic policy, when the center of gravity in economic policy shifted away from the minister of planning in the Castelo Branco government, Roberto Campos, toward the new minister of finance in the Costa e Silva government, Antonio Delfim Neto. The new policies placed more emphasis on GDP growth than on containing aggregate demand; the prospects for their success were improved by the existence of spare capacity in the economy, especially in manufacturing industry, after the 1964–1967 stabilization program.

The first important change in the new government's external economic policy concerned exchange rates. Before 1968, the high domestic inflation rate, which was well above the inflation rates of Brazil's commercial partners, combined with a fixed nominal exchange rate adjusted through infrequent but large devaluations, produced large variations in the real exchange rate. The new policy of very small devaluations, introduced in August 1968, stabilized the real exchange rate by adjusting the cruzeiro-dollar rate by the approximate difference between inflation in Brazil and that in the United States. Although one of the aims of this new policy was to eliminate incentives for short-term speculative movements of capital, it seems to have contributed decisively to making Brazil's economy more open to foreign trade. The share of foreign trade in economic activity increased after 1968 because the uncertainty felt by economic agents, especially exporters, declined.[2]

The resumption of economic growth after 1967 caused the current-account balance to deteriorate in 1968 despite the high rate of export growth. The government's concern about the balance of payments and about pressures from sectors that had lost protection in 1967 were probably the reasons behind a partial retreat from liberalization in 1967. At the end of 1968 tariffs were again increased, although not to levels comparable to those before 1967.

Balance-of-payments pressures began to decline after 1968. Although the strong growth of exports played a part in this decline, its main cause was the behavior of the capital account. Until 1968 net capital inflows into Brazil had never exceeded US$300 million a year; between 1969 and 1973 they averaged US$2.5 billion a year. These flows, unprecedented in Brazil's economic history, were partly responsible for certain institutional and legal reforms, among them Resolution 63 of the central bank, enacted in August 1967.[3] Because capital inflows after 1968 greatly exceeded Brazil's foreign-exchange needs as represented by the deficit in the current account, Brazil's foreign-exchange reserves increased rapidly.

The disappearance of balance-of-payments constraints permitted a gradual, selective liberalization of imports. The style of economic management practiced by the government seems to have been decisive in this process. Instead of formally reducing tariff barriers and other obstacles to imports, as in 1967, the government allowed the increase in imports to be brought about more by bureaucratic methods than through the market. The Industrial Development Council (CDI) or the Tariff Policy Council (CPA) often granted requests for partial or total exemptions from tariffs on capital goods and intermediate goods.[4]

The significance of this method of increasing imports lies in the fact that tariff reductions were made de facto and not de jure. The machinery for the administrative control of imports was not dismantled, and the tariff actually paid on a given imported product could vary considerably, depending on the product's final destination. An important consequence of this bureaucratic process of administering imports was increased uncertainty about the price actually to be paid in any specific transaction. Another result of this selective, administrative liberalization was that conventional estimates of protection, based on the tariffs in force, tended to overestimate the average tariff paid by importers. Even if this potential effect is ignored, estimates of the structure of effective protection in Brazil suggest that the economy was more open to imports in 1973 than before or after.

The first oil shock did not produce an immediate response in Brazil's foreign-trade policy. The initial strategy was more to finance the current-account deficit than to force the economy to adjust to the deterioration in the terms of trade. Brazil was well placed on the international capital markets to adopt this strategy, which was facilitated by the increasing availability of petrodollars from the surpluses of OPEC countries.

The increase in the current-account deficit in 1974 to US$7.1 billion, a figure four times higher than the maximum of previous years, compelled the new government to adopt measures that would reduce the deficit, not merely finance it. These measures were directed principally toward trade rather than exchange rates. The policy of minidevaluations continued; but the real exchange rate hardly altered, despite the sharp fall in the terms of trade. The first steps were taken in June 1974; central bank Resolution 289 suspended the financing of all products subject to tariffs of 55 percent or more; and this measure was accompanied by Decree-Law 1334, which doubled tariffs on almost 900 products deemed to be superfluous. Throughout the rest of the year additions were made to this list, and tariff reductions on capital goods were eliminated.

Restrictions were tightened in 1975 as deposit requirements were established for many categories of imports. In July a compulsory 100 percent deposit, to be repaid after six months without any monetary adjustment or interest, was introduced. At the same time, the incentive system for exports of manufactures was expanded. The principal incentive program was the Special Program of Fiscal Incentives for Exporters (BEFIEX), which became increasingly important after 1975. The financing of exports, linked to the value of the firm's exports in the previous year, was introduced in January 1975.

Although the increase in exports was greater than the cutback in imports, as the government seems to have recognized at the time, it is difficult to regard as liberalization measures the steps taken to increase exports after 1974. The reform efforts, undertaken in the 1960s, had reduced the antiexport bias implicit in Brazil's price structure. After 1975, however, this bias was much smaller or even nonexistent for the majority of manufactured products. The new incentives were based more on financing than were the previous measures, which had more of a fiscal character.

By 1976 there was little left of the timid, hesitant, yet significant opening of Brazil's economy to foreign trade that was a feature of the 1964–1974 period. The government had chosen bureaucratic methods to control the level of imports and increase exports. Exchange-rate policy was little used and the real exchange rate did not alter significantly in the period 1973–1979.

Analysis of the Reforms

By contrast with other countries that proceeded from the import-substitution phase of reform to a stage of greater openness to foreign trade, Brazil tried a reform of its external economic policy that did not go as far as a real liberalization.[5] Despite the tentative nature of this reform it seems worthwhile to analyze the effects of Brazil's foreign-trade policy on the economy at that time, and to examine why the attempt to open the economy to international markets ceased.

The traditional model of trade liberalization puts more emphasis on opening the domestic economy to imports than seems relevant in Brazil's case. According to the model, whose implicit premise is that the goal of policy is to keep the current account in balance, when there is a general reduction in import duties, as occurred in Brazil in 1967, preserving this balance requires a real devaluation. The devaluation improves the competitiveness of exportable products and leads to an increase in exports.

Brazil's experience departs from the traditional model in two basic respects. First, Brazil's foreign-trade policy after 1964 put more emphasis on a direct increase in exports through fiscal and credit incentives than on an increase induced indirectly through devaluation. Second, the deregulation of the capital account after 1964, and especially after Resolution 63 in 1967, led to a large surplus in the balance of payments. After 1967, therefore, any need for real devaluation of the cruzeiro was eliminated by the combination of an increase in export receipts and massive inflows of foreign capital.

The impact of these inflows, reinforced by the increase in exports after 1967, is clear in the behavior of the real exchange rate. In my study prepared for the World Bank project, this rate is defined as the ratio between the price of tradable goods, whether importable or exportable, and the price of nontradable goods and services. This second group includes most of the services and products which either by their nature or because of the effects of protection are not exported or imported by Brazil.

This relative price, P_T/P_N, plays a fundamental role in Brazil's external equilibrium. A nominal devaluation, or an increase in the cruzeiro cost of a dollar, raises the price P_T of tradable goods in relation to the price P_N of nontradables. Domestic inflation tends to increase P_N more than P_T, since P_T is more closely linked to international prices. On the production side, a real devaluation, or an increase in the ratio P_T/P_N,

FIGURE 3.1   The Real Exchange Rate, January 1964–February 1987

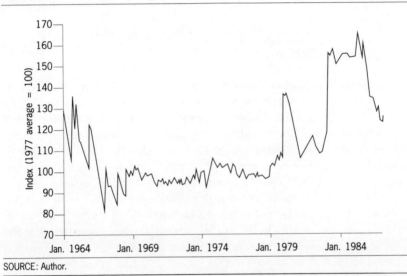

SOURCE: Author.

increases the output of tradable goods, whether exports or import substitutes, and in the long run stimulates investment in these sectors. On the consumption side, the increase in P_T/P_N tends to reduce the consumption of tradable goods. Both effects, whether on production or consumption, help to improve the current-account balance.

Figure 3.1 shows the monthly change in the real exchange rate P_T/P_N throughout the period from January 1964 to February 1987.[6] An increase in the rate represents a real devaluation, hence an increase in Brazil's competitiveness in the international market. The impact of the minidevaluations policy adopted from August 1968 onward is clearly apparent in the reduced fluctuations in the real exchange rate. This new exchange-rate policy did not bring about any decline in the real exchange rate, which remained relatively stable for more than a decade.

With respect to foreign-trade policy, the most striking aspect of Figure 3.1 is the absence of any real devaluation in the period of greatest openness to imports, between 1967 and 1974. As we have seen, the impact of capital inflows after 1967 made it possible for imports to rise without any need for a real devaluation of the cruzeiro. Even though the Brazilian government emphasized exports from 1964 onward, the increase in exports was achieved despite the real exchange rate and not because of it.

Another aspect of Brazil's experience evident in the behavior of the real exchange rate is the lack of any significant exchange-rate response to the first oil shock in 1974. The real exchange rate remained relatively constant throughout the 1970s despite the sharp fall in the terms of trade. This overvaluation of the cruzeiro in real terms after the oil shock clearly reflects the government's decision to control foreign trade through administrative measures rather than to use exchange-rate policy and take steps that would affect the current account deficit.

In retrospect, one can see that Brazil lost certain opportunities to increase its competitiveness on international markets during the period 1968–1974 because it deregulated capital flows but was at the same time too timid in liberalizing imports. The short-term stability of the real exchange rate, one of the aims of the new exchange-rate policy in 1968, did not theoretically exclude a gradual real devaluation between 1968 and 1974; but in practice real devaluation was ruled out by the massive capital inflows that began at the end of the 1960s.

The reasoning pursued here assumes a significant reaction by producers to changes in relative prices, such as the real exchange rate, P_T/P_N. One possible explanation why Brazilian governments in the period 1968–1979 preferred to control foreign trade by administrative measures lies in uncertainty about the price elasticity of exports. In the first years of the post-1964 regime, this attitude partly reflected the fact that Brazil's exports were still dominated by primary products, whose price elasticity on world markets was relatively small. This position of uncertainty was to some extent supported by the state of imports as well. The products still imported by Brazil, after more than a decade of import substitution and the almost complete elimination of imports of consumption goods, were essential products whose price elasticity was also low.

The growing importance of manufactures in the domestic product and in Brazil's exports since the late 1960s, however, calls into question this pessimism about the effectiveness of relative price changes in restoring equilibrium to the current account.[7] Although price changes may have a relatively small impact on certain traditional primary products, a number of estimates of the response of Brazil's manufactured exports suggest that their price elasticity is relatively high. Among such studies should be mentioned the estimate by Cardoso and Dornbusch (1980), which showed that exports of manufactures responded significantly to relative prices, which included the nominal exchange rate, incentives for exports of manufactures, and domestic and external prices. An attempt to reassess this hypothesis using new data and techniques produced an even higher estimate.[8]

Estimates of Brazilian producers' response to prices are important for the design and execution of foreign-trade and exchange-rate policies. If the response is indeed significant, as these estimates suggest, exchange-rate policy would be at least as effective in its impact on the current-account balance as the complex system of administrative controls used by the Brazilian government in recent decades.

Up to now our discussion of Brazil's foreign-trade policy from 1967 through 1974 has been confined to the question of its relationship to the external equilibrium, but this policy also had an important internal dimension. The resistance to greater liberalization of the economy is based, in Brazil as elsewhere, on a concern that price changes brought about by a significant degree of reform would have negative effects on production and employment in sectors facing stiff competition in the external market. The probability that these effects will occur depends critically on the flexibility and mobility of factors of production. In the textbook models, where prices are flexible and production factors perfectly mobile between sectors, exposing the economy to international prices immediately produces greater economic efficiency, through the movement of resources into activities in which their real return is maximized. Since these models have always been received with a certain skepticism in Brazil, it is appropriate to ask whether the country's experience with trade liberalization in the period 1964–1974 revealed significant economic costs in terms of employment or other indicators of activity.

The strong expansion of production in Brazil after 1968 maintained the demand for labor and raised real wages virtually throughout the economy. Because of this aggregate effect evidence of negative effects of import penetration would be more apparent at the sector level than at the macroeconomic level; if employment grew more slowly in sectors in which imports rose more, we might conclude that opening the economy had negative though temporary effects on the level of employment. It would be difficult, however, to observe any significant effects of this kind between 1967 and 1974, even if they actually existed. Table 3.1 contains data on the increase in imports in ten sectors of manufacturing industry, according to the Brazilian Institute of Geography and Statistics (IBGE) classification.[9] Since everything grew during this period, not only imports but also employment and output, the relevant variable for measuring the penetration of imports in industry is the ratio of imports to output by sector. The percentage increase, or $\hat{I}$,[10] in this ratio between 1967, the year of tariff reform, and 1974 is shown in the first column in Table 3.1. In nine of the ten sectors the imports coefficient rose, and in some cases it doubled.

The second column in Table 3.1 shows the percentage increase in employment by sector. As one would expect, employment increased significantly in almost all sectors as a result of the large rise in output during the period. The increases by sector, however, do not seem to show any negative correlation with the increase of the imports coefficient. This impression is confirmed by a regression which aims to relate the change in employment by sector ($\hat{I}$) to the change in the imports coefficient ($\hat{E}$):

$$\hat{E} = 91.53 - 0.041\ \hat{I}$$
$$R^2 = 0.002 \quad F(2.8) = 0.018$$

TABLE 3.1   Import Liberalization and Employment in Manufacturing, 1967–1974

	$\hat{I}$ (percentage increase in imports/output ratio)	$\hat{E}$ (percentage increase in employment)
Nonmetal mineral products	23.4	67.4
Metal products	236.6	88.0
Machinery	69.0	271.6
Electrical and communications equipment	45.7	85.6
Transportation equipment	87.9	55.8
Paper and cardboard	179.4	69.0
Rubber	109.8	101.6
Chemicals	53.8	41.1
Textiles	115.6	22.2
Food products	–42.9	77.2
SOURCE: Author.		

If greater penetration by imports were associated with a smaller increase in employment, the coefficient $\hat{I}$ would be significantly negative. Although the estimated coefficient has the expected negative sign, the equation is totally lacking in explanatory validity, as is shown by the coefficient R^2 and the statistic F.[11] Our results show that increased import penetration into Brazil throughout the period 1967–1974 produced no significantly negative effects on the level of employment.

Lessons of the 1964–1974 Experience

Brazil's experience in economic liberalization between 1967 and 1974 suggests some observations that are relevant to a discussion of foreign-trade policy. In retrospect, the episode is seen as a mixture of success and failure. Despite some suggestions that there was actually no liberalization and that the tariff reductions in 1967 were merely cosmetic, the increase in imports in relation to output shows that the reforms had a significant impact, especially in manufacturing industry. The absence of any relationship between import penetration and employment by sector suggests that the liberalization policy achieved without significant short-term costs the long-term advantages of resource allocation provided by greater integration into the world market.

If the liberalization experiment was a success, it is reasonable to ask why it ended in failure. The answer appears to lie in two areas: (1) the bureaucratic manner in which the policy was conducted, especially from 1969 onward, and (2) the lack of coordination with exchange-rate policy.

The expansion in Brazil's foreign trade was basically administered by the government and not by the market. Although the level of protection fell, the government retained wide discretionary powers over exports and imports. Brazil's current foreign-trade policy appears to be a legacy of this approach. The practice of liberalizing imports through exemptions conceded on a case-by-case basis, without any changes in formal structures, has enabled a strong bureaucratic control to be maintained down to the present. Up to 1974 this bureaucratic power was used in a liberalizing manner; thereafter it was easy to use it to curtail imports.

The price that the Brazilian economy paid and is still paying for this method of administering foreign trade is a notable increase in costs and in the uncertainty associated with each transaction. It has been mentioned in this chapter that the lessened uncertainty about the real exchange rate after 1968 seems to have had beneficial effects on foreign trade; it would be strange if the uncertainty the present system has created about tariffs did not also have its own, adverse, effects. The opacity of a complex, discretionary system also permits bureaucratic abuses, as was observed by the former director of CACEX (Foreign Trade Department, Bank of Brazil), Dr. Benedito F. Moreira (1988):

> Rather than a customs tariff, Brazil has a system of administrative control and a vast, highly bureaucratic structure for granting benefits on a case-by-case basis, which delays urgent and priority investments and, paradoxically, makes them more expensive. Our customs policy has ceased to be a tool of economic policy, in the sense of an instrument for the balanced protection of national output, and has become a perverse form of state intervention in the economy and of the exercise of power.

The second major lesson of the events of 1964–1974 is the importance of coordinating foreign-trade policy and exchange-rate policy. As this discussion has shown, the liberalizing reforms at the end of the 1960s were undermined by massive financial capital inflows after 1968. In the absence of other changes, the liberalization of imports would have led to a real devaluation, which would have increased the competitiveness of Brazil's exports. Instead, the cruzeiro remained overvalued in real terms until the end of the 1970s.

In present-day Brazil capital inflows on a scale comparable with those of the late 1960s are very improbable. From the standpoint of exchange-rate policy and its effect on exports, this lack of new capital, paradoxically, is good news. The evidence available suggests that the response of Brazil's exports to the real exchange rate is strong enough so that the country can rely more on exchange-rate policy and less on the administrative control of foreign trade.

Notes and References

Notes

1. Between 1967 and 1974 exports increased by value at an average annual rate of 25 percent; between 1974 and 1985 this figure fell to 11 percent.

2. A microeconomic and econometric analysis of the effects of the minidevaluation policy on increasing exports is given in Coes 1979.

3. Resolution 63 allowed a Brazilian bank or other authorized agency to borrow money on the international market for onlending to local firms. The final borrower bore the exchange risk. Another significant factor at that time was the low real interest rates on the international market.

4. Among other agencies authorized to grant exemptions were SUDAM (Superintendency for the Development of the Amazon Region) and SUDENE (Superintendency for the Development of the Northeast).

5. The countries of the Southern Cone, especially Chile, and certain countries in Asia have gone significantly farther in opening their economies to the international market.

6. The data used to calculate P_T/P_N were the general price index in Brazil and the U.S. wholesale price index, which was used to approximate the prices of the products figuring in international trade. For a discussion of the calculation technique, in which P_N is obtained as a residual, see the main study (Coes 1990).

7. This attitude, known in English as "elasticity pessimism," seemed to receive some support from the first econometric studies of the effects of prices on foreign trade. Later studies tended to raise estimates of elasticities considerably.

8. See Cardoso and Dornbusch 1980. The revised estimate is presented and discussed in the main study (Coes 1990).

9. In five other sectors data on production and employment exist, but the level of imports is not significant. These sectors are wood products, furniture, clothing and footwear, beverages, and tobacco products.

10. This variable is defined as

$$\hat{I} = \frac{[(M/P)_{74} - (M/P)_{67}]}{(M/P)_{67}}$$

(M represents imports, and P represents penetration.)

11. The statistic t of the coefficient is only 0.134, totally insignificant.

References

Cardoso, E., and R. Dornbusch. 1980. "Uma equação para as exportações brasileiras de produtos manufaturados." *Revista Brasileira de Economia*, April–June.

Coes, D. 1979. *The Impact of Price Uncertainty: A Study of Brazilian Exchange Rate Policy*. New York: Garland.

———. 1990. "Brazil." In *The Experience of Brazil, Colombia, and Peru*. Vol. 4 in Liberalizing Foreign Trade, ed. D. Papageorgiou, M. Michaely, and A. M. Choksi. Oxford: Basil Blackwell.

Moreira, B. F. 1988. Article in the *Folha de São Paulo,* January 12.

Argentina: Trade Reform, 1976–1982

Argentina's economic performance from 1860 to 1929, while it followed an export-led growth strategy, was impressive. By contrast, stagnation and high inflation became endemic under the import-substitution model followed after the Great Depression. In the late 1970s, Argentina made a move to liberalize trade and financial policies; but, unfortunately, the mismanagement of the transition from a highly distorted to a free-market economy led to an external crisis. The inconsistent use of policy instruments is evidenced by the excessive overvaluation of the Argentine peso that prevailed after 1976, a phenomenon which cannot be blamed on trade liberalization itself but must be ascribed to inconsistent accompanying policies. Within five years the reversal of liberalization policies had begun.

In this chapter I focus on this major liberalization attempt and the reasons for its failure, paying particular attention to the timing and sequencing of trade liberalization and the role of accompanying policies.[1]

A Frustrated Move toward Liberalization

In March 1976, a military government took power in Argentina, and the appointed economic team, led by José Martínez de Hoz, started what can be considered the first and only significant attempt at trade liberalization in Argentina's history.

By the 1970s, Argentina was a repressed economy, both commercially and financially. This condition, far from being new, was almost

FIGURE 4.1   Foreign and Domestic Terms of Trade, 1913–1984

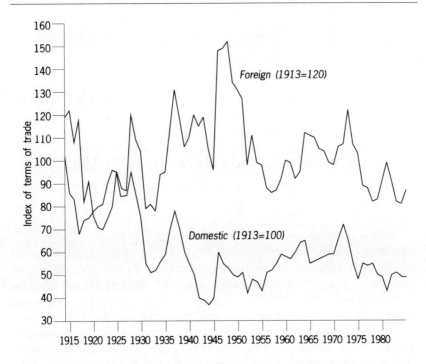

SOURCE: Cavallo and Cottani 1990, fig. 1.5.

chronic, as can be inferred from Figure 4.1. The data reveal that more than fifty years earlier, domestic terms of trade were systematically lower than external terms of trade. This difference was the outcome of implicit or explicit taxes on trade arising from import and export restrictions. Trade was not, however, the only activity to suffer economic repression; financial policy was similarly repressive. Domestic interest rates had low ceilings, and the government intervened directly in credit allocation. High inflation produced negative real interest rates, with a consequent decline in money demand, as illustrated in Figure 4.2. Inflation, in turn, was high because of very large and persistent fiscal deficits financed by creating domestic credit (see Figure 4.3).

The Martínez de Hoz administration (1976–1981) was firmly committed to economic liberalization and to the particular goal of reversing the excessive government intervention that had characterized economic policies for several decades. In April 1976, immediately following the military coup, controls on domestic prices were eliminated. Exchange-rate unification was achieved by the end of 1976, and the black market

FIGURE 4.2   M1 and M3 as Proportions of GDP in Current Prices, 1913–1984

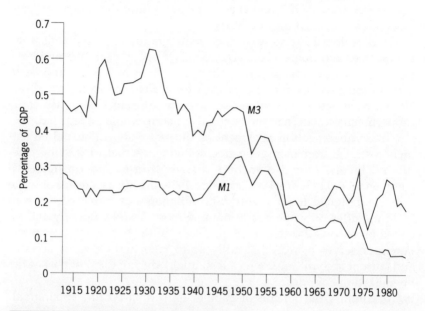

SOURCE: Cavallo and Cottani 1990, fig. 1.6.

FIGURE 4.3   Ratio of the Fiscal Deficit to GDP, 1913–1984

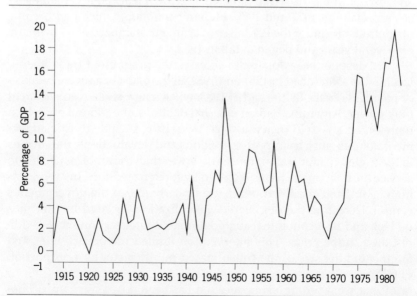

SOURCE: Cavallo and Cottani 1990, fig. 1.7.

then disappeared. The financial reform of June 1977 lifted ceilings on domestic interest rates. Taxes on traditional exports were practically eliminated during 1977, and the capital account of the balance of payments was opened at the end of 1978.

Import liberalization was much more gradual and discriminatory, but the trade account reached record levels of openness in 1979 and 1980. During those years, most quantitative restrictions had been eliminated, and, for most sectors, nominal tariffs were at their lowest historical levels. Tariff reduction was intended to continue up to 1984, when some proportional escalation in the nominal structure would be retained.

Trade liberalization in Argentina did not entail the usual adjustment costs. Far from increasing, unemployment actually fell to unprecedented levels. Nor did income-distribution goals conflict with commercial policies. Real wages fell in 1976, mainly as a result of wage controls designed to cope with high inflation, but increased again in 1979 and after, as wage policy became more flexible. Initially, the increase in imports did not create problems in the balance of payments. Foreign reserves increased steadily up to 1980, and the trade account and current account improved substantially during the first part of the liberalization episode.

In contrast, the benefits of trade liberalization became apparent almost immediately. Productivity increased in agriculture and manufacturing, and consumers benefited from lower prices of tradable products. Investment rates were relatively high during the liberalization period; and, except in the 1978 recession, GDP growth reached acceptable levels, especially in 1977 and 1979. Endemic inflation, which had become uncontrollable under the Peronist government, stabilized at a lower rate for several years and began to fall in 1980.

Yet, despite these apparent successes the program of trade liberalization was abandoned in 1981 and 1982, in the midst of a severe balance-of-payments crisis. By the end of 1983, when a new civilian government took power, Argentina had an external debt of some $45 billion, which represented a sixfold increase since 1975–1976. Despite drastic adjustment policies, such as import restrictions and devaluations, the surplus in the trade account was significantly lower than the amount needed to service the debt on the terms required by foreign creditors. Inflation was high again, and the fiscal deficit was clearly out of the government's control. Defeating the objective of liberalization declared by Martínez de Hoz and his economic team, government intervention increased in response to the crisis. This intervention limited import activities and augmented the size of the consolidated public sector as a proportion of GDP.

What went wrong? This question has been posed by many economists puzzled by Argentina's unusual experience. Most sensible explanations focus on macroeconomic policies that led to excessive real appreciation of the peso. During the episode of trade liberalization, several attempts were made to reduce inflation. Domestic macroeconomic policies were geared to this objective rather than to the needs of the trade liberalization program. Real appreciation was the direct consequence of the lack of coordination among the fiscal, monetary, and exchange-rate policies used to disinflate; however, as I will argue, the timing and sequencing of liberalization reforms may also have been a source of undesired fluctuations in the real exchange rate.

The Stylized Facts

Crucial features of the Martínez de Hoz stabilization-cum-liberalization episode were:

- Export liberalization came before and was more extensive than import liberalization.

- Destabilizing capital inflows took place mainly as a result of external borrowing by the public sector.

- Stabilization policies were based first on monetary contraction and then on the use of the nominal exchange rate as an active anti-inflationary instrument, with virtually no fiscal discipline.

Trade policies. The program of trade liberalization was a two-stage reform. During the first stage (1976–1978), commercial policies relied more heavily on export liberalization and export promotion than on competitive tariff reduction. It was only during the second stage (1979–1981) that tariffs were allowed to fall competitively, albeit in a gradual and discriminatory fashion.

The principal measure taken by the new authorities was to eliminate taxes on traditional exports. These were of two kinds: explicit taxes or *retenciones*, set at levels as high as 50 percent for cereals and 59 percent for oil seeds; and implicit taxes levied through the multiple-exchange-rate system, which was highly biased against traditional exports. Both taxes disappeared in 1977, the first gradually, as retenciones were reduced, and the second soon after the unification of the exchange rate. Nontraditional exports, on the other hand, received larger subsidies under the new regime. These subsidies, especially the financial incentives for export promotion (*prefinanciación* and *financiación*) rose significantly between 1977 and 1981.

The administration decreed the first tariff cut in November 1976. The policy of tariff reduction continued in 1977, intensifying during the second semester, and was implemented without preannouncement. The general consensus among economists is that these tariff cuts merely reduced the redundancy in existing protection. Nevertheless, the first stage of the trade liberalization program also eradicated most of the import licenses and prohibitions which had proliferated under the previous regime. The second stage consisted of a five-year program of preannounced, quarterly tariff reductions beginning in January 1979. This program was too gradual and did not treat industries uniformly; moreover, departures from the preannounced schedule created uncertainty. Whereas the first stage fulfilled its objective, the second stage of trade liberalization was aborted.

On the whole, trade liberalization proceeded slowly. In 1980, the level and variance of tariffs and other taxes on imports were still high.

Capital inflows. Like other South American countries, Argentina received an influx of foreign capital during the late 1970s. This influx was fostered by domestic policies and by international financial conditions, as the oil-price booms of the 1970s created buoyant conditions in international financial markets. On one hand, oil exporters accumulated large surpluses, which were channeled to capital-starved nations. On the other hand, that real interest rates were negative provided an incentive to borrow abroad. Many developing nations responded to this incentive, and Argentina was no exception. In Argentina as in other countries, however, domestic policies helped to transform an otherwise healthy opportunity into an overborrowing crisis.

The capital account has been disaggregated in Figure 4.4 to distinguish between private- and public-sector flows. Inflows of private capital surfaced at two different times during the liberalization episode: from the third quarter of 1977 to the second quarter of 1978 and from the second quarter of 1979 to the first quarter of 1980. In contrast, the public sector was a net borrower during almost every quarter in the years 1976–1981, especially in the last two years of that period.

Exchange-rate policy. It is possible to distinguish between two periods, in which different exchange-rate policies were applied. From the last quarter of 1976 to the end of 1978, the government followed a crawling-peg rule by which expected inflation and changes in the level of reserves influenced the rate of the crawl. In January 1979, government officials introduced a downward crawling peg based on the preannouncement of future rates of depreciation. To induce a fall in inflationary expectations, the crawl was made to decrease gradually. Forthcoming changes in exchange rates, called a *tablita*, were preannounced daily: the govern-

FIGURE 4.4   Capital Flows, 1976–1981

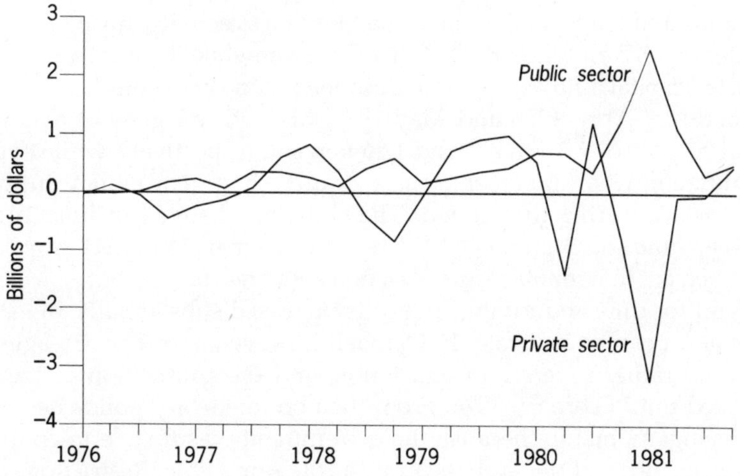

SOURCE: Cavallo and Cottani 1990, tables 3.29 and 3.30.

ment pegged the nominal exchange rate at specified future times and committed itself to adhere to preannounced values.

When an unscheduled 10 percent devaluation took place in February 1981, the government preannounced a new tablita, pre-fixing the nominal exchange rate until the month of August. This time the announcement lacked credibility, and the government was forced to devalue again in March (30 percent). The active crawling peg was then abandoned.

Monetary policy. The financial reform of June 1977 eliminated the ceilings on loan interest rates charged by the banking system, as well as those paid on savings and time deposits. Banks also became free to choose their customers without the intervention of the central bank or other government agencies, and liberal entry regulations were established to encourage competition in the financial sector. Real interest rates climbed from negative to positive levels, helped by the credit demand of the public sector, which became a strong customer of commercial banks.

Before the reform, monetary policy was not an active instrument of stabilization but simply followed price increases. Only the sources for expanding the monetary base changed, as domestic sources (government deficit financing, rediscounting, and so on) became less important than foreign sources (changes in international reserves) derived from current-account surpluses that had begun to accumulate since 1976. Immediately after the reform, the money supply was contracted in order to deflate. As a consequence of contraction, loan interest rates nearly doubled in nominal terms and led to a fall in investment and less activity during the last quarter of 1977 and the first half of 1978. Meanwhile, high interest rates attracted capital inflows, which undermined monetary control.

Between April 1976 and May 1977, M1 and M3 grew at average monthly rates of 9.7 percent and 12.6 percent, respectively, while average inflation was 6.6 percent. These figures show that money supply was passive during this period. The situation changed in June 1977. Between June and September 1977, the rate of expansion of M1 dropped to 4.2 percent in nominal terms (–3.6 percent in real terms); but, since the demand for time and savings deposits increased substantially, M3 still grew at a positive real rate. In October, however, all monetary aggregates fell rather severely in real terms; and the contraction of credit persisted until February 1978. From then on, monetary policy became passive again, mainly because the government was unable to control money supply and the exchange rate at the same time. Restrictions on capital mobility were eliminated in 1979. When the government started to pre-fix nominal exchange rates in the presence of free capital mobility, money supply became endogenous (the stock of reserves was the adjusting variable). The central bank set as a target for domestic credit expansion in 1979 a rate (70 percent) that was more or less consistent with the preannounced rate of devaluation (65 percent). The actual growth of domestic credit, however, was 130 percent, mainly because of a significant reduction in the minimum reserves ratio required on all kinds of deposits from an initial level of 45 percent in December 1977. Reserves fell throughout the second semester of 1978, most steeply during the last quarter; in December of 1978 the ratio was 16.5 percent. Lack of monetary discipline remained a keynote of policy in 1980, when domestic credit grew by 90 percent while the exchange rate was devalued only 25 percent. This time, however, the source of monetary expansion was a large fiscal deficit, part of which was financed by the central bank.

Fiscal policy. According to official publications of the Argentine government, the deficit of the public sector fell from 14 percent of GDP in 1975 to 9.8 percent in 1976 and to 3.2 percent in 1977. This reduction was achieved mainly through increased tax collection. Current spending fell during the same period, but this decline was matched by a rise in public investment. Between 1977 and 1981, current spending increased again; and, despite a fall in public investment and a further increase in tax collection, the deficit doubled as a proportion of GDP. This measurement of the deficit does not include payments of interest, either real or nominal, on domestic and foreign public debt. The inclusion of payments at the real interest rate would not, however, alter the picture substantially.

FIGURE 4.5   Fiscal Deficit and Source of Financing, 1970–1982

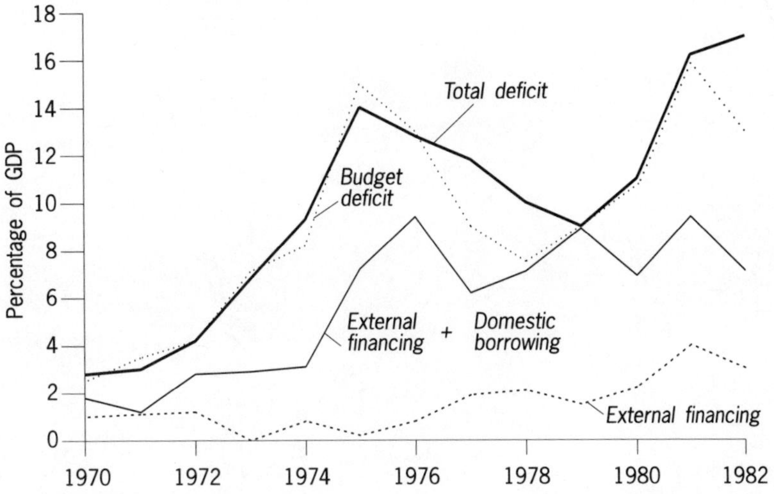

SOURCE: Cavallo and Cottani 1990, fig. 4.2.

An alternative measurement of the deficit is derived by lumping the different sources of financing together. This is shown in Figure 4.5 using an unofficial estimation by Cavallo and Peña (1983). Note that the higher values of the total deficit are due to (1) the influence on domestic public debt of nominal-interest-rate payments, which are elevated in a world of high inflation; (2) the inclusion of the extrabudgetary or central bank deficit as a component of the total deficit; and (3) the use of different methodologies to calculate the deficit (the Secretaría de Hacienda uses data on public revenues and expenditures, whereas Cavallo and Peña look at the overall increase in public debt). The nonbudgetary or central bank deficit results from a wide range of transactions in which the monetary authority engages—such as foreign-exchange operations, credit subsidies through rediscounting facilities, interest payments on bank reserves, and financial assistance to rescue private firms from bankruptcy—which are also a part of the consolidated government deficit but were not included as such in official statistics.

Reversing the Real Appreciation

Figure 4.6 shows the changes in the real bilateral exchange rate of the U.S. dollar between 1975 and 1984. After a short period of real depreciation in 1975 and part of 1976, the RER (real exchange rate) started to fall

---

FIGURE 4.6   Real Bilateral Exchange Rate, 1974–1985 (U.S. dollar)

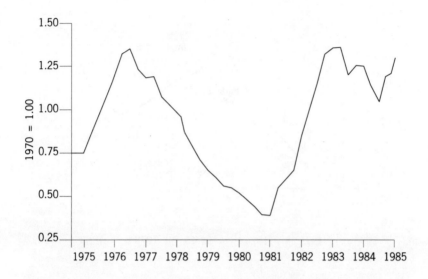

SOURCE: Cavallo and Cottani 1990, fig. 4.5.

---

in the fourth quarter of 1976. Real appreciation lasted until February 1981, when the first discrete devaluation in five years took place. Between the first quarter of 1981 and the first quarter of 1983 the RER increased in real terms by a factor of three, reversing the previous trend. This wide fluctuation in the RER is the most remarkable aspect of this period.

It is worthwhile to examine the changes in the real exchange rate in relation to a basket of currencies, to determine whether the real appreciation of the Argentine peso was equally significant when measured against this yardstick. This question is important, because the dollar had been depreciating against the deutsche mark, the pound, the yen, and other hard currencies until the end of the 1970s.

In Figure 4.7, the real bilateral exchange rate (the RER) and the multilateral exchange rate (RERM) are plotted. The multilateral exchange rate is a trade-weighted average that includes the currencies of countries with which Argentina has maintained significant trade flows. As expected, RERM is higher than RER after 1976; however, the difference between the two rates narrows from the middle of 1978 until it practically disappears at the point of maximum real appreciation in the first quarter of 1981. In consequence, the total appreciation of the real exchange rate between the fourth quarter of 1976 and the first quarter of 1981 is roughly the same for both the RER and the RERM.

FIGURE 4.7   Real Multilateral Exchange Rate, 1975–1980

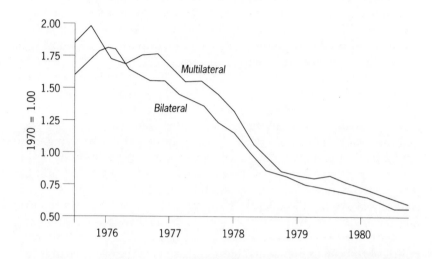

SOURCE: Cavallo and Cottani 1990, fig. 4.6.

The determinants of real-exchange-rate behavior. Exchange rate policies are not sufficient to explain why the Argentine domestic currency
appreciated so much from 1977 to 1981. The indices in Figures 4.6 and
4.7 represent a real variable, the value of which cannot be determined
entirely by movements in the nominal exchange rate. In fact, changes in
the real exchange rate are closely related to changes in commercial policies, capital flows, and fiscal or monetary disturbances.

An important element in the initial appreciation of the peso between 1977 and 1978 was the elimination of export taxes. To the extent
that a fall in the real exchange rate simply represents a movement toward a new equilibrium consistent with fewer trade distortions, it does
not lead to currency overvaluation. A problem arises, however, as the
fall in the real exchange rate reduces the profitability of those tradable
industries which do not benefit directly from the reduction in export
taxes. This problem is not essentially different from the "Dutch disease"
caused by a significant increase in the foreign price of enclave export
goods, except that here the source of real appreciation is domestic rather
than foreign.

In Argentina, export liberalization induced a significant increase in
agricultural production. Because of this sector's response, the trade balance improved substantially; and, since import liberalization was slow,
export surpluses were monetized. Real appreciation reduced the competitiveness of nontraditional exports, inducing fresh distortions as

export subsidies were used to keep effective exchange rates high. At the same time, the low real exchange rate created a disincentive for foreign investment because foreign investors received fewer pesos per dollar in real terms. Moreover, the real appreciation favored activities such as tourism abroad by Argentine citizens and importing of contraband (smuggling), further complicating the process of opening the economy and stabilizing the balance of payments. These problems could have been avoided if imports had been liberalized along with exports.

To assess the relative importance of trade and accompanying policies in explaining real appreciation, Cottani and García (1987) used quarterly data to build a simple dynamic model of real-exchange-rate determination and then ran simulations under alternative policy scenarios. According to their results, export taxes, capital inflows, and the mix of monetary and exchange-rate policies account for about 65 percent of real appreciation between the last quarter of 1976 and the first quarter of 1981, each factor having almost equal weight in explaining this variation. They also concluded that if trade, fiscal, and financial policies had been implemented more consistently, the real exchange rate would have stabilized near its 1970 level (see Figure 4.8). Consistent implementation would have avoided the sharp U-shaped fluctuation experienced during the decade following 1976. Under these conditions, the antiinflationary program would have been successful, and the trade and financial reforms would have transformed the previously repressed economy into a free economy without giving rise to exaggerated costs during the transition.

FIGURE 4.8   Actual and Simulated Real Exchange Rate, 1976–1985

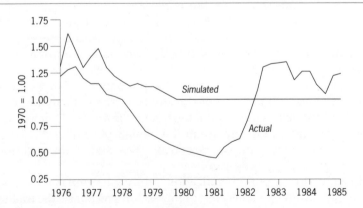

NOTE: Period represented extends through first quarter of 1985.
SOURCE: Cavallo and Cottani 1990, fig. A.3.5.

A more consistent trade policy would have allowed a greater increase in imports during 1977 and 1978. More imports would have avoided the accumulation of surpluses in the current account that resulted from the combination of export liberalization and promotion. To achieve the increase, the tariff program should have been implemented earlier and more rapidly. On the other hand, the expansion of domestic credit should have been more in accordance with the rate of pre-announced devaluation in 1979 and 1980. Such expansion would have required a reduction in the fiscal and quasi-fiscal deficits. Finally, the capital account should have been opened only after fiscal equilibrium had been reached and inflation had been brought under control.

Note and References

Note

1. A full discussion is contained in Cavallo and Cottani 1990.

References

Cavallo, Domingo, and Joaquín Cottani. 1990. "Argentina." In *The Experience of Argentina, Chile, and Uruguay*. Vol. 1 in Liberalizing Foreign Trade, ed. D. Papageorgiou, M. Michaely, and A. M.Choksi. Oxford: Basil Blackwell.

Cavallo, Domingo, and Angel Peña. 1983. "Deficit fiscal, endeudamiento del gobierno y tasa de inflacion: 1940–1982." *Estudios* (IEERAL [Instituto de Estudios Economicos sobre la Realidad Argentina y Latinoamericana], Córdoba, Argentina), no. 26.

Cottani, Joaquín, and Raúl García. 1987. "Real Appreciation and the Order of Trade and Financial Liberalization: Argentina 1976–81." World Bank, unpublished.

Chile: Trade Liberalization since 1974

Like many developing countries, Chile has had a long tradition of protectionism toward manufacturing; and this protectionism intensified after the Great Depression of the 1930s. Postdepression growth, based on an import-substitution strategy and well sheltered behind high trade barriers, became dependent on the roller coaster of copper prices and soon lost momentum as a consequence of a very limited domestic market and increasingly inefficient additional import substitution. Aware of some of the basic shortcomings of the protectionist policy, three governments made modest attempts to liberalize in the 1950s and 1960s; unfortunately, all failed. Unlike many countries in similar circumstances, however, Chile went on to mount a very ambitious project of trade liberalization between 1974 and 1979. This major effort unified exchange rates; eliminated import prohibitions, export quotas, tariff exemptions, and nontariff barriers; and reduced to a flat 10 percent a tariff schedule that had been widely dispersed around an average of 90 percent. This last liberalization experience has been successful. It has survived a major depression—the most severe since the 1930s—and it has withstood appreciating real exchange rates, dumping practices, and protectionist policies in world markets. Chile's reform also withstood the domestic financial crisis and even the traditional rent-seeking lobbies which had been so successful in the past. It is true that the trade policies suffered from some adjustments between 1962 and 1988; however, the rules established after 1974, in essence, have not been altered.

How did trade liberalization occur in Chile? What were the issues that affected policy making during the process of liberalization? What worked and what went wrong? Why was liberalization sustainable? All are questions that will be addressed succinctly in this chapter. The answers should suggest some lessons for other countries attempting to liberalize trade.

Stabilization and Reform, 1974–1979

When the Pinochet government took over, in late 1973, the economy was a shambles. Aggregate production had declined precipitously in 1972 and 1973; decapitalization had accelerated in numerous sectors; inflation had jumped far above any previous levels; and shortages of goods had developed at the retail level, while barter and generalized black markets disrupted normal distribution channels even more seriously. Foreign reserves had become volatile despite a sizable increase in foreign debt between 1970 and 1973. The fiscal deficit surpassed 20 percent of GDP in 1973. Real income gains achieved in 1971 had been eroded and even reversed; and the drain of capital and of technical and managerial expertise had accelerated, further reducing the supply of these essential resources. The economic decline was exacerbated by a drop in world copper prices and by the withdrawal of traditional sources of international credit.

The new authorities were intent on carrying out major changes. Their economic goals, in September 1973, were meant to be consistent with a social and institutional framework radically different from its predecessor. The system had to achieve effective economic decentralization before political decentralization and an efficient democratic mechanism could be implemented. The market was to be the principal instrument of economic initiative with the private sector as a privileged agent of development. Initially, the government had two primary economic objectives: achievement of a high and stable growth rate with full employment, and eradication of extreme poverty. The chaotic situation it faced, however, required the government to make the elimination of macroeconomic disequilibria another major objective. Finally, the opening of foreign markets was to be instrumental both in exploiting comparative advantage and in achieving greater efficiency in domestic production. For the purpose of opening these markets, a major trade-liberalization effort began in 1974.

In early 1974, all quotas and official approvals required to initiate an import operation were eliminated.[1] The 187 tariff positions directly prohibited were reduced to only 6 in 1976, and the 10,000 percent prior deposits that had been required on more than 50 percent of the tariff positions were eliminated before the end of 1976. Tariffs, ranging from 5 percent to 750 percent, were adjusted to reach a uniform 10 percent in June 1979, five and a half years after the trade liberalization started.

Tariff adjustment was done in three stages. The first stage lasted from the beginning of 1974 until mid-1975. During this period, the maximum tariff came down from 750 percent to 120 percent, the simple average tariff dropped from 105 percent to 57 percent, and the modal tariff declined from 90 percent to 55 percent. Between mid-1975 and mid-1977, the second stage, tariffs were adjusted so that the schedule would vary between 10 percent and 35 percent, with a simple average of 19.7 percent and a mode of 15 percent. This tariff scale was applied according to the degree of processing; and, during the adjustment process, tariffs were reduced in a linear fashion. During the final stage, which lasted about a year and a half (December 1977 to June 1979), tariffs were reduced on a monthly basis to reach the single 10 percent rate. Only automobiles and other vehicles were exempted from the 10 percent rule.

Two basic complementary measures also were taken: at the outset of the liberalization efforts, a consumption tax was imposed on all goods, imported or domestically produced; and most duty exemptions, which affected about 50 percent of imports, were eliminated before December 1979. Only those exemptions corresponding to international agreements remained—with a few others that, on the whole, represent minor exceptions. Even capital goods, which had been legally exempted from customs duties, were subject to the general rule, although duties could be paid in several annual installments.

As this discussion has suggested, trade-liberalization efforts were carried out in the midst of a major attempt to reduce inflation and reorganize the economy as a market system. At the same time, the liberalization efforts were facing the unexpected and dramatic impact of a major recession in 1975. Restrictive fiscal and monetary policies were implemented as part of the effort to stabilize the economy. Deficit spending by the central government was ended in 1976, and fiscal deficits were fully eliminated by 1979. Similarly, the exchange rate was used from 1976 to 1982 to slow down inflation, while wage adjustments were directed toward the same goal, at least until 1979. The recession of 1975 added its depressive effects on income and employment to the expected difficulties of implementing stabilization policies. After 1978, however, inconsistent wage and exchange-rate policies were carried out. Such policies, on top of large increases in expenditures stimulated by over-optimistic expectations and financed by a significant inflow of foreign credit, kept pressure on prices and thereby put off the desired outcome. Nevertheless, inflation decreased from about 750 percent at the end of 1973 to about 10 percent in 1982.

Along with stabilization policies, massive institutional changes ensured the desired framework for development. Price controls, multiple exchange rates, and interest-rate ceilings were eliminated to improve resource allocation. Most discrimination among productive sectors was significantly relaxed. To encourage saving and investment, interest rates were freed; quantitative and qualitative controls over credit were removed; barriers to new local banks were reduced; and banking regulations on minimum capital, reserve requirements, and ownership concentration were eased. Although the financial market was gradually opened after 1977, controls on capital flow remained until mid-1981. Also, a more flexible foreign-investment code was introduced to guarantee equal treatment of national and foreign investors. Consistent with the desire to reduce the size of the public sector and to improve its efficiency, personnel was significantly reduced, public enterprises became self-financing and enjoyed pricing freedom, and more than 500 state-controlled firms were privatized. Finally, a major reform in 1978 secured a significant degree of liberalization of the labor market.

Only general and largely qualitative conclusions can be drawn from analyzing the impact of this liberalization. It is difficult to isolate the effects of trade policy from those of other contemporaneous policies and external shocks. Nevertheless, analysis of these impacts may elicit useful observations and conclusions, and our aim will be necessarily modest. Three areas of economic activity have been chosen in which to evaluate the effects of liberalization: trade, production, and employment. Some of the effects were consistent with expectations and show the successful side of Chilean trade liberalization. Others, unfortunately, imposed costs. Both benefits and costs will be summarized in the next two sections.

Successes of Trade Liberalization

Exports increased regularly in real terms between 1973 and 1979, both in constant prices (averaging 8 percent a year) and as a share of GDP. The real exchange rate remained during this period at a higher average level than during previous decades, even though it declined steadily from 1976. Relatively low wages, large increases in port efficiency, and administrative expediency also supported export activities; and external conditions were favorable to nontraditional Chilean exports. During this period, too, investment became increasingly concentrated on exportables, and relative prices were more favorable than they had been to exports. How much of the overall success in exports can be assigned to liberalization policies and how much to exogenous circumstances is difficult to know. Further, exports were significantly diversified as nontraditional exports were stimulated along the lines of comparative advantage provided by the traditional export, copper. Nontraditional exports related to copper grew from 2.7 percent of total exports in the period 1971–1973 to 34.7 percent in the years 1980–1981.

Imports also grew significantly between 1973 and 1979; however, the impact of trade liberalization was small, despite the large reductions in tariffs. On the one hand, import-competing sectors were much less protected than they appeared to be, since the first steps of the liberalization came in the midst of a great recession. On the other hand, the massive increase in imports that occurred after 1977 was influenced greatly by the large increase in demand financed by foreign indebtedness. Both factors were unrelated to the policy of trade liberalization. Since both exports and imports increased with liberalization, the economy steadily became more open, as expected. Imports of consumption goods increased relative to imports of other categories. This change in composition was expected, because the majority of manufacturing production in Chile before 1974 was in automobiles, the most protected sector. Agricultural imports, on the other hand, became more concentrated in cereals, for which Chile had the least comparative advantage.

The GDP grew at an above-average rate during the period of trade liberalization, with the exception of 1975 (during the recession). It is difficult to show, however, that the policy impact on the GDP was positive. At most, perhaps it can be argued that the impact was not negative. Liberalization policy had a large delayed impact on the composition of output, as expected. Although the proportion of tradables did not increase, the composition of this category changed drastically in favor of subsectors with comparative advantage, such as forestry, fruits, fishing, and industries making intensive use of abundant natural resources—industries such as pulp and paper, furniture, ferromolybdenum, and fishmeal. The exportable sectors increased their production as expected. Some substitution of capital for labor also occurred. The substitution was very significant in manufacturing and may have been caused by changes to product lines more attractive as exports and more competitive with imported products, as well as by the introduction of new technologies in anticipation of changes in relative prices. The industrial sector, previously highly protected and old-fashioned, was fundamentally modernized as a consequence of substituting capital for labor, with obvious positive results that lasted beyond the liberalization episode.

The dynamic effect of liberalization in manufacturing could have been produced by changes in the size and number of firms in the sector, new technology, product composition, and so on. This effect was positive during the period of liberalization and was particularly large afterward; however, it was outweighed in most industrial subsectors by the negative impact derived from tariff reduction. The share of industry in GDP fell from 25 percent to 21 percent.

Finally, the impact of liberalization on employment overall was positive, despite its negative effect on manufacturing. This result goes against the general view that liberalization must have a negative impact. This view is tautological, however, in the sense that it is usually confined to the analysis of highly protected sectors, which obviously lose from liberalization. When we consider sectors that may gain with liberalization—in Chile, some parts of agriculture, forestry, fishing, and nontradables, for example—then the results are totally different. Labor moves from one sector to another, or among subsectors. Still, such movement of labor into the growing sectors in so short a time—within five years—comes as a surprise. Further, although employment has been expanding in manufacturing since 1979, it has been increasing even faster in agriculture. The downward historical trend of employment in that sector has been reversed, and rural-urban migration has even stopped. Liberalization has stimulated the development of activities highly intensive in natural resources. A side impact of that development has been decentralization of economic activities to locations where the resources are found. Previously declining cities such as Copiapó, Rancagua, Curicó, Temuco, and Coyhaique are growing quickly now.

What Went Wrong?

Trade liberalization had some negative impacts and was followed by a period of acute crisis. It should be made clear at the outset that the crisis was not born of trade liberalization; nevertheless, main features of the crisis should be described. Showing the difficulties through which the liberalization policy had to go will lead to a better understanding of the policy's depth, penetration, and relevance.

The trade balance was no doubt a main worry for Chilean authorities, facing a closed international capital market when the trade liberalization policy was initiated. The depletion of foreign reserves then could be considered undesirable. In that respect, liberalization appears to have been relatively unsuccessful despite the flourishing of exports. The trade balance, usually positive, was negative between 1976 and 1982; and the deficit increased substantially in 1980 and 1981. Not too much should be made of this feature up to 1979, however, since the imbalance was of limited size; imbalances in succeeding years were more worrisome. Several qualifications serve to some extent to separate the behavior of the trade balance from trade liberalization. The results observed were influenced greatly by relatively buoyant demand and by production conditions increasingly financed by a significant increase in foreign indebtedness, a fall in the terms of trade, and an appreciation of the real exchange rate. This variety of influences makes it difficult to tie the worsening of the trade balance unequivocally to liberalization, and it is likely that the relative influence of trade liberalization was rather limited.

The negative impact of trade liberalization on production and employment is probably the main issue in this discussion. In Chile, it was concluded—even postulated—that trade liberalization would lead to general unemployment. It was shown in the preceding section of this chapter that liberalization did not have this effect, even during such a limited time as the period of trade-policy implementation (1974–1979); the effect is even less evident if a longer period is observed. Some amount of unemployment was unavoidable, since the reduction in tariffs had greater effects on the most protected subsectors of the economy, all of which belonged to manufacturing and most of which were highly inefficient and unable to face even modest competition. The sectors producing goods that could be replaced by imports—six of the seventeen subsectors—suffered a very large cut in production; production and employment also fell in most other nonexport-producing sectors, but by more modest amounts. As expected, however, production and employment increased in subsectors producing exportable and nontradable goods. Unfortunately, these subsectors did not carry the greatest weight in the industrial sector during the period analyzed. Another way to present these conclusions is to underline the fact that the production and employment impacts of liberalization were negative and important in those subsectors that enjoyed the highest nominal tariff protection when the process of liberalization was initiated, whereas the effects were positive and large in those subsectors with the lower initial tariffs.

This mixed result hides a major problem of the fractional joblessness arising from the significant reduction in manufacturing employment, caused, in turn, by external shocks and stabilization policies coming at a time of very large, overall unemployment. Although sector-specific unemployment was compensated for by greater employment in other sectors, in the short run, workers could not adapt their skills overnight to transfer into the exportable sectors.

Why Was Trade Liberalization Sustainable?

During the decade that has elapsed since liberalization was implemented, the policy has been subjected to strong attacks. Apart from a few concessions—which, in my view, have not affected the fundamentals—the trade liberalization appears to have resisted these pressures successfully.

The first pressure with which the policy had to contend was the erosion of competitiveness of both exportables and import substitutes. This erosion was a consequence of the systematic and prolonged appreciation in the real exchange rate between June 1979 and mid-1982. Large capital inflows—created when the abundant availability of credit in world financial markets met the unsatisfied demand for domestic credit—financed rapidly growing consumption and investment expenditures. Prices of nontradables were pressed upward; but prices of tradables remained constant, since the exchange rate was fixed. Consequently, the real exchange rate kept falling until capital inflow dried up and the currency was devalued; both events took place in mid-1982. The extent of reduction in the real exchange rate—about 20 percent—was sufficient to eliminate the existing nominal protection for importables in 1979 and to reduce substantially the direct benefits for exportables that had been provided by the combination of tariff and exchange-rate policy since 1974. Both sectors suffered a severe blow as a consequence of this reduction. Production and employment in manufacturing were reduced further, by 5 percent and 4 percent, respectively between 1979 and 1981. This result implied that the impact of the real exchange rate on manufacturing added two significant costs to those generated by trade liberalization. Both of these costs were thought to result from the trade-liberalization policy. However wrong, this position contributed to many pressures against this policy.

The policy also had to contend with the international recession that began in 1980. Transmitted to the Chilean economy through reduced demand for its exports, increased international interest rates, and a liquidity squeeze in international financial markets, the effects were profound. Production plunged; unemployment jumped from 11.2 percent in 1980 to 23.7 percent in 1982; and the economy had to reduce consumption and investment appreciably—more than 20 percent—to adjust its current-account deficit.

Not surprisingly, the 1982 recession eroded the government's political power. High unemployment and reduced real wages substantially weakened the political base; bankruptcies and high indebtedness created a rift between the entrepreneurial community and the executive branch of government. The repercussions were felt in internal pressures brought to bear against the liberalization policy: while workers and entrepreneurs saw an opportunity in the political weakness of the government to regain privileges and franchises lost during liberalization, officials sought to exploit that vulnerability to rebuild their own political support. At the same time, the commercial policies being adopted by trading partners facing their own shortages of foreign currency were renewing internal protectionist pressures. Consequently, entrepreneurial organizations campaigned to protect their markets from foreign competition.

In the face of these considerable pressures for renewed protection, the actual changes in trade policies made since liberalization seem remarkably moderate. The tariff policy in effect since June 1979 has been subject to two types of modification: changes in the level of the uniform tariff and the application of countervailing duties.

The uniform 10 percent tariff established in 1979 remained unaltered until June 1983, when it was increased to 20 percent. In September 1984, a new minister of finance decided to increase the uniform tariff from 20 percent to 35 percent—and to devalue the domestic currency by 23.6 percent. These policies were received with disapproval by a large section of the population, including most manufacturers. Thus, the tariff reduction announced by another minister of finance in early 1985 was fully endorsed by June of that year; and the tariff returned to 20 percent, where it remained until January 1988. Since then, the uniform tariff has been reduced to 15 percent. The discussion of this issue has faded, although supporters of tariff differentiation have not abandoned their efforts. Some surcharges have been applied in agreement with GATT to counter specific cases of dumping, but they have been firmly restricted to a few products. These surcharges also were defined in such a way that the basic tariff plus the surcharge did not exceed 35 percent. The application of surcharges has not opened the door thus far to general tariff increases.

Most countries facing such a deep recession, a huge balance-of-payments problem, and a growing protectionist lobby would have gone much farther in reinstituting protection; this is what has happened in most other Latin American countries. One reason these pressures were resisted in Chile is the determination of most Chilean ministers of finance to maintain the policy unaltered. Only one new finance minister (appointed in 1983) modified the tariff policy, and his increases (in 1983 and 1984) were reversed by a successor. The tenacity of the policy makers kept trade liberalization in place long enough for groups that had a vested interest in defending it to develop. Reversal would financially damage those groups, which have reoriented their resources toward the objectives of liberalization. Specifically, since a new group of producers was created in the export sector, exports have diversified significantly, the absolute number of exporters has increased enormously, and substantial investment has been made in the exportables sector. For this new group, a reversal of the tariff policy would bring unfavorable relative prices; consequently, its members make their opinions felt when changes in policy are discussed.

In Chile, liberalization has been maintained long enough to bring about a complete reorganization of production structures in the import-substituting sectors. Lines of production unable to compete with imports disappeared; new lines and products developed according to the new set of relative prices, and resources were invested in modernizing several plants. A reversal in the tariff policy today would obviously impose high costs on the firms that adjusted to new policies. By the same token, most old firms that might have benefited from a reversal have disappeared, leaving as potential beneficiaries only a few producers of import substitutes who might obtain rents.

The reasons described in the preceding two paragraphs may go a long way toward explaining why the tariff change enacted in 1983 was mild and why the larger increases in 1984 did not last more than six months. Another reason for the durability of the policy was the increasingly successful behavior of the trade balance. A relatively stable macroeconomic policy framework, which kept domestic expenditures consistent with the foreign-exchange restriction, has been supported by an exchange-rate policy directed toward maintaining or surpassing the high level reached by the real exchange rate in 1983 and 1984. The resulting growth in the trade balance, together with the stability of foreign-exchange reserves, has limited the pressures to use tariff accommodations to adjust the trade balance. Yet another reason for the durability of the liberalization policy is that the organizations representing entrepreneurial interests, after almost ten years of debate, have failed to reach an agreement on a new tariff schedule to be proposed to the government. Such disunity among entrepreneurs comes from the conflict between those favoring low tariffs—mainly exporters and merchants—and others—mainly rent-seekers in the importables sector. The durability of trade liberalization in Chile has been increasingly ensured because sustainability breeds on itself. Conversely, it becomes increasingly difficult to reduce tariffs the longer they remain in force.

Lessons of Chilean Liberalization

This final section selects some of the lessons drawn from Chile's experience that would be relevant to trade reform in other developing countries. The order of presentation has no particular bearing upon their relative importance.

The lifting of quantitative restrictions (QRs), numerous and significant in many developing countries, may induce an abnormally high demand for imports and diminish credibility with respect to the policy's permanence. After the period of adjustment, however, demand for import growth will return to lower levels. Containing import increases may require an exchange rate higher than would be needed in the long term under the given tariff regime, although borrowing from abroad can be more efficient in containing these increases. A high exchange rate will stimulate exports at the beginning of the liberalization process and can be retained when further liberalization measures, requiring appreciation of the appropriate exchange rate, are taken in subsequent stages. To avoid any major impacts from QR elimination on the trade balance and relevant exchange rates, it probably would be wise to reduce QRs by stages and according to a predefined schedule.

A separate stage for QR replacement seems necessary to establish relative prices, since awareness of these is important to both policy makers and firms. Policy makers need to know the price or tariff equivalence of QR barriers to determine liberalization's quantitative targets, its adjustment costs, and its expected benefits, duly balanced by political considerations. It would be impossible for authorities to reach even a rough estimate of the figures on which to base reasonable decisions, if protection were reduced directly in a situation where either nontariff barriers prevailed or tariffs offered protection in excess of the price difference between local and importable goods. Private firms, for their part, need to understand the impact of policies to make decisions on resource reallocation. This is true even if the only liberalization policy in question is the elimination of QRs, and understanding this impact is a more difficult task when substitution of tariffs for QRs is only one among many other market-oriented economic policies, such as elimination of price controls, ending of all sorts of subsidies, and tax reform. The Chilean experience suggests that liberalization should start with the elimination of QRs and other gross distortions such as multiple exchange rates, before tariff reduction is considered.

There was also a special stage at the beginning of Chile's liberalization process in 1974 when commercial policies were normalized, by eliminating tariff exemptions and defining tariff rules for capital goods that had been imported tariff-free in the past, and when other policies for exports and imports were specified. All of these steps were important, because they tended to put all potential exports and imports on the same footing at the outset and because the elimination of import exemptions fostered interest in opening the economy still further.

Successful liberalization requires successful exports. The behavior of exports was crucial in the success of the liberalization episode in Chile; however, it was not the result of a special policy phase designed for that purpose. Rather, Chilean experience demonstrates that beyond setting the stage for export promotion, it is necessary to create the basic conditions that underlie successful exporting. The most important requirements are reducing antiexport bias and establishing a real exchange rate consistent with liberalization and the trade balance. In addition, both conditions should be kept relatively stable over time. The prior elimination of QRs is another important condition for success, since producers will feel more secure with less government intervention in exports and imports. Further, since without QRs prices will more accurately reflect their real value, resources will flow more easily toward sectors with greater comparative advantage, and growth potential will be improved. An important caveat should be added, however. The

Chilean experience indicates that a high real exchange rate cannot be maintained artificially for long periods of time, since the government cannot control the price level unless tariffs are reduced permanently. It follows that a significant reduction in tariffs should be coupled with exchange-rate management consistent with the trend of the trade balance during liberalization and after.

Large fiscal deficits may place severe hurdles in the way of any serious stabilization attempt. The resulting high rates of inflation may hide significant alterations in relative prices, dislocating markets and leading to inappropriate decisions on the allocation of resources. These trends certainly do not contribute to a proper framework for liberalization. Stabilization policies do not appear to pose any significant problem for the appropriate sequencing of trade liberalization. They may pose a major problem for its success and sustainability, however, if the exchange rate is used as a stabilization instrument to affect price expectations, as is likely to happen. Fixing the exchange rate subjected trade liberalization in Chile to considerable strain between 1979 and 1982, since there was little downward flexibility in prices and employment and production fell, with obvious and immediate social and political consequences. This policy of using the exchange rate as an instrument of stabilization is unfortunate at any time during episodes of trade liberalization; so if a choice is possible, it would be better to implement a major trade-liberalization policy after overvaluation derived from stabilization policies has finished.

Perhaps more important than the stabilization and sequencing of liberalization is getting the prices right. Coherent and relatively stable prices are probably the best environment for liberalization. Moreover, the appropriate combination of wages, exchange rate, and interest rate is vital. Each one should be directed toward adjusting the market for which it is relatively more efficient: wages for the labor market, exchange rate for the foreign-exchange market, and interest rate for the credit market. If the exchange rate is fixed exogenously and the interest rate also is given from the outside, then the only tool left to adjust the three markets, in case of disequilibrium, is the wage rate. Eliminating other adjustment tools places an excessive burden on the wage rate and transmits the wrong signals to the labor market, as well. This is what happened in Chile between 1979 and 1982. Adjustments to increasing disequilibrium in both trade balance and credit markets were expected to come from significant downward adjustment in nominal wages—an impossible task, since it had no political support. Accumulation of foreign debt substituted for wage adjustment.

In Chile, employment was affected by trade-liberalization policies, although, according to the results of our analysis, aggregate employment was not negatively affected. Employment is probably the most sensitive issue associated with liberalization policies, in particular with the pace of their application. As a whole, in Chile, employment tended to increase in the trade sector, which includes both exportables and importables. This trend was concomitant with a major change in the composition of employment: work was reduced among importables but increased among exportables. This optimistic result hid a major problem, frictional unemployment arising from the significant reduction in manufacturing employment produced by liberalization and by external shocks and stabilization measures occurring at a time of very large overall unemployment. Although sector-specific unemployment was offset by greater employment in other sectors, workers could not adapt their skills overnight to transfer into the exportable sectors. This short-term dislocation does not prompt the conclusion, reached by some analysts, that trade liberalization created unemployment and lost production. These adjustment costs should be considered more than redressed by changes in the structure of production consistent with improved resource allocation, quality changes, and modernization in the trade sector. Even if the future development of the industrial sector is less labor-intensive than in the past, liberalization policies will have been justified in the long run by higher productivity in manufacturing and other sectors, as well as by greater growth potential and higher development of other labor-intensive sectors. Furthermore, unemployment in manufacturing (and mining) in Chile was more than offset by labor absorption in agriculture, so the net impact was positive, even at first. Perhaps one way to face this issue is to help the firms affected by liberalization reduce their costs of adjustment.

A conclusion similar to that on the elimination of QRs applies to the sequencing of any other policies that may be expected to have significant impacts on resource allocation—such as the freeing of prices, the elimination of subsidies, and increased market orientation of the economy (such as that which occurred in Chile after 1973). All of these measures preferably should be carried out (as they were between 1974 and 1979 in Chile) before, or together with, the application of the trade-liberalization policies, for the sake of keeping the decisions on resource allocation consistent with the liberalization policies. Although the essence of the arguments in this chapter is that everything else ideally should be done before the trade liberalization, it should be added quickly that the appropriate political timing for the liberalization could evaporate in the meantime.

One important lesson of the second episode is that liberalization policies acquired more strength and support, and became more sustainable, as consumers and producers became increasingly aware of their benefits. The direct beneficiaries of these policies proliferated to include public enterprises; some import-substitute producers, whose effective protection was higher than before; producers of nontradables; and exporters, whose lobby grew stronger as exports diversified. The united opinion of officials responsible for most macroeconomic policies and for the public institutions of Chile—that liberalization was needed—further strengthened the credibility of the policies in the eyes of both producers and consumers.

Notes and Reference

Notes

I am indebted to Sergio de la Cuadra for his useful comments on this analysis. This chapter is based on de la Cuadra and Hachette 1990.

1. More than 50 percent of tariff positions had been subject to official approval.

Reference

de la Cuadra, Sergio, and Dominique Hachette. 1990. "Chile." In *The Experience of Argentina, Chile, and Uruguay*. Vol. 1 in Liberalizing Foreign Trade, ed. D. Papageorgiou, M. Michaely, and A. M. Choksi. Oxford: Basil Blackwell.

Greece: The First Reform Attempt, 1953

Greece's first postwar attempt to liberalize foreign trade occurred in April 1953. The actions taken at that time were a clear departure from the strongly protectionist practices of the earlier period.

Economic Conditions before 1953

Despite the devastation of World War II and the subsequent civil war, the Greek economy recorded modest improvements in the last half of the 1940s. Substantial American aid, first under the Truman Doctrine and subsequently under the Marshall Plan, helped repair the ravages of the wars by providing funds for investment and for imports of basic goods, materials, and machinery. Up to 1951, in fact, foreign aid made up for virtually all of the government's annual budget deficits. In the years before 1953, as Table 6.1 shows, aid funds exceeded by far Greece's annual earnings from commodity exports.

In fiscal year 1951–52 the United States considerably reduced its aid to Greece and notified the Greek government that U.S. aid would be terminated within the next few years. The centrist government in power felt compelled to take strong measures to lessen Greece's dependence on foreign aid. To reduce the budget deficit the government imposed special taxes on real estate, on firms that borrowed from banks, and on high-income professionals. The Greek government also reduced administrative costs, imposed a freeze on government hiring, abolished certain subsidies to consumers, and suspended payment of the usual

TABLE 6.1   Foreign Assistance from Marshall Plan and Mutual Security Agency,
               1949–1953 (millions of U.S. dollars)

Year	Foreign assistance	Merchandise exports	Trade balance	Ratio of foreign assistance to merchandise exports	Ratio of foreign assistance to trade balance
1949	212.8	83.4	−284.2	2.55	0.75
1950	263.6	85.1	−312.6	3.10	0.84
1951	206.8	101.9	−329.7	2.03	0.63
1952	182.0	114.3	−160.4	1.59	1.14
1953	81.2	134.1	−109.2	0.61	0.74

SOURCE: Kottis 1989, t. 2.1.

Easter bonus to labor (a bonus equivalent to half a month's salary). These measures considerably improved the budget situation, and by 1953 the government's ordinary-budget and total-budget deficits (the total budget includes public investment) had dropped sharply as percentages of GNP (see Table 6.2).

The effects of the highly contractionary policies, together with a big drop in agricultural output caused by unfavorable weather and normal crop cycles, led to a real GDP stagnation in 1952. Manufacturing output declined in real terms, and growth in mining and in the services sector slowed down (see Table 6.3). There was also a drop in the real value of total gross fixed asset formation, especially in the public sector; but gross investment in manufacturing remained unchanged (see Table 6.4) It is not known whether employment was seriously affected by the austerity measures. These fiscal policies were supported by highly tight monetary measures.

Trade Policies before Reform

On the eve of trade reform in 1953, the main instruments for the promotion of exports and for the control of imports were

- Tariffs. The tariff structure in effect had been established in 1923. Table 6.5 presents estimates of average tariffs and excise taxes, based on ninety-three major categories of goods.

- Special import levies. Special levies on imports were imposed on a total of sixty-two categories of goods, at rates ranging from 25 to 150 percent of c.i.f. price. In Table 6.6 are

TABLE 6.2   Main Monetary and Fiscal Variables, 1951–1957

	1951	1952	1953	1954	1955	1956	1957
Change in money supply, M1 (%)	22.7	10.5	46.8	18.8	23.9	12.8	18.7
Change in money supply, M3 (%)	23.4	11.1	47.1	20.3	28.5	30.5	41.1
Change in CPI (%)	12.6	5.1	9.2	15.0	5.7	3.7	2.3
Change in GDP deflator (%)	10.0	3.9	15.7	11.8	7.4	6.6	0.9
Change in lending to primary sector (%)	46.6	16.6	−2.1	30.4	17.2	16.9	21.7
Change in lending to manu-facturing and mining sector (%)	55.2	14.4	74.6	23.9	4.3	22.4	32.4
Change in lending to commerce (%)	18.2	−32.8	6.5	31.4	−0.3	58.9	22.9
Nominal interest rate on deposits (%)	10.0	8.0	8.0	7.0	7.0	10.0	9.0
Nominal interest rate on lending to industry (%)	12.0	12.0	12.0	10.0	9.0	10.0	10.0
Ordinary-budget deficit (% of GNP)	4.0	2.2	0.3	0.9[a]	0.1[a]	1.3	0.2[a]
Total-budget deficit (% of GNP)	—	5.5	3.5	1.1	1.7	2.7	2.0
Total-budget expenditures[b]	91.9	100.0	101.6	123.3	147.2	176.7	190.7
Ordinary-budget expenditures[b]	91.9	100.0	99.5	128.3	155.1	189.6	194.8
Government investment expenditures[b]	—	100.0	112.2	98.1	107.5	111.5	170.6

NOTE: Dash = not available.
a. Surplus.
b. Fiscal years 1950–51, 1951–52, 1952–53, 1953–54, 1954–55; 1951–52 = 100.
SOURCE: Kottis 1989, t. 2.2.

estimates of the average levies and standard deviations for six of these categories.

- Foreign-exchange rates. Before 1953, Greece made use of multiple exchange rates, primarily through the use of foreign-exchange certificates (FECs). These were introduced in October 1947 to assist exports and discourage imports. The Bank of Greece issued exporters certificates for the foreign exchange they had brought in. Importers could then buy foreign currency from the Bank of Greece by cashing FECs that they had obtained on their own from the exporters. FECs were abolished in June 1951.

TABLE 6.3   GDP Growth and Structure, 1951–1957

	1951	1952	1953	1954	1955	1956	1957
Real GDP growth by sector (%)	9.0	0.01	13.5	3.4	7.6	8.9	6.9
Agriculture	13.5	–5.60	25.9	–2.6	7.0	2.7	13.0
Mining	39.6	21.10	23.3	8.0	14.0	13.6	8.3
Manufacturing	6.3	–1.20	15.3	11.3	9.6	10.6	6.7
Energy	3.1	5.50	19.2	7.6	18.7	15.4	11.0
Construction	–17.1	6.70	21.8	–0.1	10.4	17.7	–0.1
Services	9.2	2.90	4.8	4.9	5.3	10.4	2.8
GDP share of major sectors (%)							
Primary sector	29.2	27.40	30.6	28.9	28.9	27.3	29.1
Manufacturing sector	11.5	11.40	11.6	12.5	12.8	13.0	13.1
Rest of secondary sector	6.9	7.30	7.9	7.8	8.2	8.8	8.7
Services	52.4	53.90	49.9	50.8	50.1	50.9	49.3

SOURCE: Kottis 1989, t. 2.4.

TABLE 6.4   Investment, Capacity Utilization, and Profitability, 1951–1957

Category	1951	1952	1953	1954	1955	1956	1957
Fixed-asset formation (billions of drachmas, 1970 prices)	15.1	14.0	14.25	14.4	16.0	19.4	19.1
Gross investment in manufacturing (billions of drachmas, 1970 prices)	3.2	3.2	2.0	1.8	1.9	2.4	2.8
Capacity utilization in manufacturing (%)[a]	51.0	46.8	53.2	58.9	63.7	68.7	70.2
Profitability of net capital invested in the nonagricultural private sector (%; excludes dwellings)[b]	—	—	—	10.3	12.2	13.4	13.1

NOTE: Dash = not available.
a. Estimated from data on capital stock and production in the manufacturing sector.
b. Ratio of business profits to fixed plus circulating capital.
SOURCE: Kottis 1989, t. 2.5.

TABLE 6.5   Prereform Tariffs and Excise Taxes, 1953

Import groups	Average tariff (percentage of c.i.f.)[a]	Average excise tax (percentage of c.i.f.)
Consumer products	35.6	18.4
Intermediate products	25.8	13.7
Capital products	16.1	11.7

NOTE: The average tariff for all categories was 29.8 percent. The average excise tax was 13.6 percent. All estimates are based on actual tax collection at customs for 1952.
a. Price including cost, insurance, and freight to destination.
SOURCE: Kottis 1989, t. 2.6.

TABLE 6.6   Special Levies on Imports, 1953

Import groups	Number of goods in group	Average levy (%)	Standard deviation
Consumer products	6	141.6	47.7
Intermediate products	5	90.0	51.7
Capital products	51	95.0	49.5
Agricultural products	35	105.7	41.8
Mining products	20	95.0	51.7
Manufacturing products	7	78.5	54.7

NOTE: Average levy (simple, unweighted) for 62 categories was 99.2 percent. Standard deviation was 49.85.
SOURCE: Kottis 1989, t. 2.7.

- Quantitative restrictions (QRs) and import licensing. All of Greece's imports were subject to strict licensing up to 1953. QRs were applied to imports of machinery competing with domestic production and to imports of consumer goods other than those satisfying the "basic needs" of the population. Such goods were specified by the Council of Foreign Trade, made up of cabinet members.

- Bilateral trade agreements. The Greek government signed several bilateral trade agreements after World War II. In 1953, Greece had such trade agreements with several communist countries as well as Brazil, Egypt, Finland, and Israel. Bilateral trade expanded in 1952, when it accounted for 2.1 percent of imports and 5.1 percent of exports.

- Direct export subsidies. Introduced after World War II for some goods, by 1953 these subsidies covered a total of thirty-five categories of products and were used together with special import levies to reduce the trade deficit. The rate of subsidy ranged from 15 to 50 percent of the f.o.b. (free on board) price. In Table 6.7 are estimates of average subsidy

TABLE 6.7   Direct Export Subsidies, 1953

Export groups	Number of goods in group	Subsidy rate (%)	Standard deviation
Consumer products	15	31.6	9.2
Intermediate products	15	44.0	8.3
Capital products	5	44.0	5.5
Agricultural products	6	24.1	6.6
Mining products	15	44.0	8.3
Manufacturing products	14	39.8	7.3

NOTE: Average subsidy for 35 categories was 23.8 percent. Standard deviation was 10.2.
SOURCE: Kottis 1989, t. 2.8.

rates and standard deviation for various goods categories affected by this measure.

- Indirect export incentives. These, which had been used before World War II, increased in number and coverage after the war. The indirect incentives as of 1953 included (1) temporary exemption or refund of import duties and other taxes on imported raw materials, fuel, and packaging materials used to produce exports; (2) exemption from the turnover tax on revenue from goods exported directly by producers or exported indirectly through prior sale to domestic firms that subsequently exported them; (3) refunding of turnover tax paid on domestic manufactured and handicrafts products used in the production of exports; (4) easier terms of bank credit and lower interest rates for export trade than for import and domestic trade; (5) a reduction in the fees required by the Piraeus Port Authority if exports were being shipped; (6) easier customs procedures for exports.

The Nature of the Trade Liberalization of 1953

Facing the prospect of serious balance-of-payments difficulties as foreign aid was phased out, the Greek government decided to move quickly toward a policy of trade liberalization. On the evening of April 8, 1953, the government announced that, effective the next morning, April 9, it would implement the following measures:

- Devaluation of the currency from fifteen drachmas to the U.S. dollar to thirty drachmas to the dollar and an end to multiple exchange rates.

- Abolition of special levies on imports and of direct export subsidies. Regular tariffs, excise taxes, and some indirect export incentives, however, were preserved.

- Elimination of licensing and quantitative restrictions on most imports. Imports of certain luxury goods still had to be licensed, as did some imports (mainly capital and intermediate goods) produced domestically. Imports of such capital goods were to be licensed only when domestic production was determined insufficient to satisfy domestic demand.[1]

The government's goal was to improve economic conditions through better functioning of markets. In short, reform was intended to bring about a modernization of the Greek economy and to promote economic development. The government believed that it had created the necessary preconditions for the success of the trade reform and was planning to continue to adopt measures for monetary and fiscal stability so that these reforms would have a lasting effect on the economy instead of bringing the merely temporary relief of previous attempts.

There is no evidence that a division existed within the Greek government concerning the new policy, the implementation of which was entrusted to the minister of coordination[2] and the minister of commerce. Furthermore, there was no debate in parliament or any other discussion with opposition parties before announcement of the liberalization measures, since they were introduced suddenly in one simple sweep overnight. The political balance of power in the parliament was such that the government could afford to pursue its policy without much concern about the opposition's views. Among the opposition, the largest left-wing party, the Union of the Democratic Left, and the smaller left-of-center parties criticized the devaluation as excessive and asserted that it was bound to raise the cost of living of the poor and to generate unfair gains. The criticism of the nonleftist opposition parties was mild, however. Newspapers of the period show that the Association of Hellenic Industries, the Athens Chamber of Commerce and Industry, the Confederation of Professions and Small-Scale Industries, and other associations praised the new measures and pledged to support the government. A week after announcement of the new policy, discussion of it disappeared from the headlines.

To prevent the prices of basic consumer goods from rising abruptly as a result of devaluation, Greek authorities instituted several temporary measures. A large portion of the government's stocks of basic commodities was liquidated to keep their prices from rising sharply. The government subsidized imports of certain foodstuffs and raw materials until July 1953; and, until December 1953, export levies were imposed on a few agricultural products widely consumed domestically (for example, olive oil, rice) to prevent their domestic prices from rising to the levels of world prices. The U.S. government assisted this effort by supplying US$35 million in basic foodstuffs. Selective price controls were imposed to ease the transition to the new price level. Finally, windfall gains on export shipments made before the devaluation, became payable to the government.

Existing controls on foreign-exchange transactions, particularly on the export of Greek capital, were preserved. Meanwhile, inflows of foreign capital were encouraged through Legislative Decree 2687. The decree provided that the fiscal regime in effect at the time foreign direct investments were undertaken would remain effective for up to ten years. The decree also established a constitutional guarantee against expropriation and provided that foreigners' earnings and capital could be repatriated. Investments in Greece by Greeks residing abroad were treated as importation of foreign capital. Short-term private borrowing from abroad was not allowed, except for certain commercial credits.

The new policies remained unchanged until 1955, when tariffs on textiles were raised at the insistence of domestic textile producers. A year later the government imposed advance deposits on about ninety imported items, a scheme which required importers to deposit interest-free with the Bank of Greece an amount equal to either 50 or 70 percent of the c.i.f. value of the import, for a minimum of three months. Table 6.8 shows the number of goods subject to all the different conditions of advance deposits under this scheme.

TABLE 6.8   Number of Products in Import Tables, 1953–1975

Table	1953	1956	1958	1961	1975
P		93	92	117	376
F		10	17	31	all products not in Tables P, F-50 and F-100
F-50		58	2,000	2,000	371
F-100		31	89	118	273
A	10	9	9	40	81
B	45	45	45	45	47

NOTES: Blank cell = not applicable.
P = imports allowed on credit and without import deposit.
F = imports allowed without import deposit but not on credit.
F-50 = imports allowed with 50 to 70 percent import deposit (depending on year).
F-100 = imports allowed with 100 to 140 percent import deposit (depending on year).
A = products subject to QRs.
B = Table of QRs and licensing.
SOURCE: Kottis 1989, t. A.1.

The 1955 increase in textile tariffs and the introduction of advance import deposits were, of course, a partial reversal of the policy of trade liberalization; however, expanded access to credit from foreign suppliers made it easier to import other goods, whose tariffs did not increase then. In sum, since protection through import deposits was much weaker than the protection provided before 1953 by means of QRs, licensing, and import levies, the partial regression into protectionism between 1955 and 1958 can be characterized as fairly small.

Exports responded well to the liberalization policy. The devaluation was more than adequate compensation for the direct export subsidies previously applicable on some goods. Greece's most important exports (such as tobacco, cotton, and raisins) were not, however, eligible for direct export subsidies before the 1953 reform. Devaluation thus considerably increased their international competitiveness. From 1953 to 1955, all exports increased faster than imports. In 1955 the government introduced some new, indirect incentives to export production, probably to counter the small protectionist regression that occurred in that year. The social security contributions paid by employers in export production were reduced, and payroll taxes were abolished for producers of export products and packaging materials used for exports. The exemption from import duties of materials used for production of exports was extended to other types of charges, and the period within which a firm could claim the exemption was extended. Export firms were also allowed to deduct up to 4 percent of total gross export revenues from taxable profits. This deduction was nominally to make up for expenses incurred in penetrating foreign markets; but firms were not required to prove that the funds were spent for marketing activities or, for that matter, for any other legitimate obligation.

The Trade Increase after Liberalization

In dollar terms, the value of imports dropped in 1953, but by much less than it did in 1952. The 1953 decrease was caused not only by devaluation, but also by the contractionary effects of stabilization policies still in effect in the first quarter of 1953. In 1954 there was a big increase in the dollar value of imports, but in subsequent years the increases fluctuated in size. Import growth after 1953 was much faster than the growth of real GDP.

At the start of trade liberalization in Greece more than half of all imports consisted of intermediate goods, crude oil, and investment goods (see Table 6.9). Demand for such goods usually reflects the level of domestic economic activity more than it reflects changes in the prices of these goods. This characteristic of the demand probably helps to

TABLE 6.9   Structure of Imports, 1952–1956 (percentage of total imports)

	Intermediate inputs[a]	Crude oil	Investment goods	Consumer goods
1952	38.6	6.8	14.7	39.9
1953	38.0	5.7	12.9	44.1
1954	39.4	4.6	13.5	42.4
1955	36.1	4.3	14.0	49.0
1956	34.8	3.3	14.7	47.3

NOTE: Deviations from 100 percent yearly totals due to rounding.
a. Other than crude oil.
SOURCE: Kottis 1989, t. 2.10.

TABLE 6.10   Growth of Imports and Exports, and Openness of the Economy,
               1953–1956

Category	1953	1954	1955	1956
Growth of dollar value of imports (%)	−11.40	35.00	10.90	27.60
Growth of dollar value of exports (%)	17.30	20.00	28.30	1.50
Growth of dollar value of agricultural exports (%)	−20.60	35.40	23.60	−0.04
Agricultural exports as % of total commodity exports	83.30	84.10	92.20	90.50
Share of bilateral imports (%)	6.00	7.10	7.90	9.40
Share of bilateral exports (%)	12.10	17.90	9.80	18.80
Openness of the economy (imports + exports/GDP, in current prices)	0.22	0.26	0.27	0.27
Growth of real GDP (%)	13.50	3.40	7.60	8.90
Change in real exchange rate [Official rate x (WPI/DPI)] (%)	63.90	0.20	−4.50	0.00
Effective exchange rate for exports (drachmas per U.S. dollar of exports)	30.02	30.02	30.01	30.04

NOTE: WPI = world price index; DPI = domestic price index.
SOURCE: Kottis 1989, t. 2.9.

explain the lack of correlation between changes in value of imports and changes in the real exchange rate. After 1953 the share of consumer goods in total imports showed a distinct tendency to rise. This increase clearly demonstrates the unqualified success of the reforms and confirms that they truly liberalized trade.

The dollar value of exports increased at an accelerated rate between 1953 and 1955 (see Table 6.10) but slowed in 1956. Greece's exports continued to consist chiefly of traditional agricultural products, which accounted for more than four-fifths of total trade exports. The rest were mining and manufactured products. Strong fluctuations in agricultural production (see Table 6.3) usually cause similar fluctuations in agricul-

TABLE 6.11   The External Sector, 1951–1957

	1951	1952	1953	1954	1955	1956	1957
Imports of goods (millions of U.S. dollars, current prices)	431.60	274.70	243.30	328.40	364.20	464.70	508.30
Exports of goods (millions of U.S. dollars)	101.90	114.30	134.10	161.00	206.50	209.60	222.80
Exports/imports ratio (%)	0.24	0.42	0.55	0.49	0.57	0.45	0.44
Import penetration ratio (%)	—	17.40	11.30	14.40	14.40	17.70	17.00
Terms of trade (1970=100)	95.10	88.00	87.10	89.10	97.70	100.30	95.80
Official exchange rate (drachmas/U.S. dollars)	15.00	15.00	30.00[a]	30.00	30.00	30.00	30.00
Real exchange rate[b] (index, 1975=100)	50.00	49.20	80.40	80.60	77.00	76.90	78.30
Foreign-exchange reserves (millions of U.S. dollars)	56.20	71.90	120.60	131.50	186.80	190.10	178.90
Trade deficit (millions of U.S. dollars)	329.70	160.40	109.20	167.40	157.70	255.10	285.50
Balance on current account (millions of U.S. dollars)	7.30	18.60	41.40	−15.10	20.80	−41.40	−76.40
Net capital inflow (millions of U.S. dollars)	5.30	6.80	14.80	30.90	33.80	43.90	65.40

NOTE: Dash = not available.
a. After April 9, 1953.
b. Official rate multiplied by (world price index/Greek CPI).
SOURCE: Kottis 1989, t. 2.3.

tural exports; but since the Greek government was stockpiling several important agricultural products and selling part of these stocks abroad at later dates, changes in agricultural production and agricultural exports did not always coincide.

After 1953, the open-economy index [(imports + exports)/GDP] increased considerably (see Table 6.10). The ratio of import penetration (see Table 6.11), which dropped in 1953, rose in subsequent years.

Postreform Economic Policies and Performance

Monetary and fiscal policy. After the trade liberalization of 1953, the Greek government continued to adopt cautious monetary and fiscal policies in order to avoid inflation and problems with external payments.

Monetary policy remained closely controlled. The money supply (M3) grew in 1953 (Table 6.2), as GNP grew considerably, and again in 1955 and 1956, following the path of GNP growth (see Table 6.3). Total bank lending expanded in 1953 but then decelerated until 1956. The nominal rate of interest on loans to industry dropped in 1954 and 1955 but rose a bit in 1956 (see Table 6.2).

The government continued its efforts to balance the budget. Except in 1956, the ordinary budget (the budget without public investment expenditure) had a surplus, and the total budget deficit was a much smaller percentage of GNP than before 1953 (see Table 6.2). Government expenditures increased in 1953 and 1954, mainly because devaluation raised the prices of government purchases and because additional expenditures were needed to help earthquake victims and to meet financial commitments undertaken when Greece joined NATO in 1952. To raise additional revenue, the authorities made a vigorous effort to improve procedures for tax assessment and collection. Also, revenues increased because of substantial GNP growth after 1953.

Prices, wages, and profits. The 1953 devaluation caused prices to rise far less than the real devaluation implied (see Table 6.11). Price stability was restored in 1955 (see Table 6.12). Real minimum wages (no data on actual wages paid were available) in the industrial sector increased marginally during 1953 and 1954 but rose strongly in 1955 and 1956 (see Table 6.13).

Estimates of profitability and capacity utilization in the manufacturing sector show that both increased after 1954 (see Table 6.4). Certain industries show increases in average output per person and in the average number of hours worked per week (see Table 6.14).

TABLE 6.12   Inflation Rates in Greece and in Nine Main Trading Partners, 1951–1958 (percentage)

	Inflation rate in Greece	Average inflation rate of trading partners[a]	Ratio of Greek inflation rate to that of main trading partners
1951	12.6	10.6	1.2
1952	5.1	4.7	1.2
1953	9.2	0.8	11.4
1954	15.0	1.6	9.3
1955	5.7	2.5	2.2
1956	3.7	3.3	1.1
1957	2.3[b]	3.3	0.7
1958	1.4[b]	3.6	0.4

a. Average for Belgium, France, West Germany, Denmark, United Kingdom, Ireland, Italy, Luxembourg, and the Netherlands.
b. Index of cost of living in Athens.
SOURCE: Kottis 1989, t. 2.11.

TABLE 6.13 Increase in Minimum Wage of Males and Females in Industrial Sector, 1952–1956

	Nominal minimum wage (%)		Real minimum wage[a] (%)	
Year	Males	Females	Males	Females
1952	3.6	2.8	0.71	0.55
1953	9.6	8.1	1.04	0.88
1954	18.4	18.5	1.23	1.23
1955	25.0	22.4	4.39	3.93
1956	13.5	10.3	3.65	2.78

a. Nominal minimum wage adjusted by the consumer price index.
SOURCE: Kottis 1989, t. 2.12.

TABLE 6.14 Product per Worker and Hours Worked per Week in Manufacturing Industries, 1953–1956

	Average product per worker (1952=100)				Average number of hours worked per week			
Industry	1953	1954	1955	1956	1953	1954	1955	1956
Textiles	120	146	146	161	44.0	45.0	49.0	60.0
Food	108	129	135	139	43.0	43.0	47.0	47.2
Chemicals	113	148	157	142	48.5	47.2	47.2	47.2
Construction materials	119	131	144	152	47.0	45.0	47.2	47.2
Wood and wood products	116	140	140	179	39.2	47.2	46.4	47.2
Electric appliances	131	163	124	82	39.2	41.6	46.4	48.0
Machinery	109	115	112	122	44.0	45.0	45.0	45.0

SOURCE: Kottis 1989, t. 2.14.

Gross domestic product and investment. The GDP growth rate increased after 1953 (see Table 6.3). The manufacturing sector's rate of growth had been negative in 1952, but in 1953 it rose a dramatic 15.3 percent. Over the next few years the growth rate averaged about 10 percent per year. The real growth rates of major manufacturing subsectors were high after 1953. This growth suggests that, although some Greek producers must have been hurt by imports, the elimination of inefficient ones and the shift of resources to more productive uses benefited the Greek economy as a whole.

From 1955 on, real investments in manufacturing began an upward trend; but, in the more immediate wake of liberalization, the growth in manufacturing output was facilitated by strong increases in the rate of capacity utilization (see Table 6.4). Legislation designed to attract foreign investors did not have an immediate effect, but foreign direct investment did begin to gain momentum in the late 1950s.

Unemployment. Lack of data makes it impossible to determine unequivocally the effect of the 1953 liberalization on the Greek labor force. On the one hand, an increase in hours worked per week in manufacturing (see Table 6.14) and strong real increases in minimum wages suggest that demand for labor may have increased. On the other hand, unemployment compensation rose by about 27 percent between 1955 and 1956, possibly reflecting a gradual increase in unemployment coverage. The rise in emigration during the period cannot be attributed directly to trade liberalization, since most of the emigrants were from rural areas, whereas any negative impact of a rise in imports would have been felt primarily among urban manufacturing workers. All that can be said is that if there was an increase in unemployment it cannot have been very large.

Balance of payments, external debt, and the government budget. After the trade liberalization, increases in receipts from invisibles and net capital inflows financed Greece's trade deficits. These changes contributed to the increase in the country's foreign reserves (see Table 6.11).

It seems that the 1953 liberalization caused no budgetary problem (see Table 6.15). Despite the abolition of special import levies, total revenue from duties and other border taxes increased because of a 35 percent increase in the value of imports (measured in drachmas) in 1953. Import-related revenues also increased as a percentage of total budget revenue up until fiscal year 1954–55, when other sources started yielding more revenue. No data exist on budgetary outlays for export promotion before 1953, but in all likelihood the fiscal savings from the abolition of direct export subsidies were large. After 1953, export subsidies constitute a very small percentage of total budget expenditures,

TABLE 6.15   Government Budget Accounts Affected by Liberalization, 1950–1956

Fiscal year	Duty and import-tax revenues (millions of drachmas)	Duty and import-tax revenues (percentage of total budget revenue)	Expenditure for subsidies (millions of dollars)	Subsidy expenditures (percentage of total budget expenditures)
1950–51	1,300	17.9	—	—
1951–52	1,513	19.2	—	—
1952–53	1,628	20.3	19.1	0.24
1953–54	2,212	22.8	25.3	0.28
1954–55	2,118	18.9	19.3	0.17
1956[a]	2,249	16.2	69.1	0.50

NOTE: Dash = not available.
a. Calendar year.
SOURCE: Kottis 1989, t. 2.17.

although it is not possible to estimate the total amount of indirect subsidization of exports.

Even if all the rise in unemployment compensation is to be attributed to increased unemployment (as explained in the preceding section, it probably cannot be), the negative effect of such benefits, subsidies, and grants on the government's budget was much smaller than the positive change in import-related revenue.

Conclusions about the Liberalization Episode

The 1953 liberalization of the Greek economy was unilateral, bold, important for the economy, and sustainable. After April 1953 there were no balance-of-payments or budget difficulties, real economic growth was strong, price stability was restored, massive unemployment did not occur, and the economy did not seem to be facing any serious difficulties.   •

In many ways, Greece's trade liberalization was a remarkable episode. Reform was implemented literally overnight and had a substantial impact on the tradable sector of the economy. Practically all QRs were abolished, along with all special import levies and all direct export subsidies, and the drachma was devalued by 100 percent relative to the U.S. dollar. (See Tables 6.16 and 6.17.) This large devaluation was the only relief the reforms offered to import-competing sectors, since there was no increase in tariffs and in any other border taxes.

The trade liberalization of 1953 was more than anything else a fundamental change from a trade regime of discretion and arbitrariness to

TABLE 6.16	Chronology of Policy Changes, 1953–1954
April 1953	100 percent devaluation of drachma; abolition of most QRs and licensing requirements and of all special import levies and direct export subsidies; temporary measures to prevent excessive rise in prices
Fall 1953	tax reform to encourage investment, reduce burden on working people and professionals, improve tax assessment and collection procedures, and reduce tax evasion; enactment of Legislative Decree 2687 to attract foreign investment
Spring 1954	reduction of nominal interest rates on business loans; credit ceilings raised for certain types of loans; adoption of new drachma (equal to 1,000 old drachmas); first postwar bond issue by government
Fall 1954	tax revision to increase tax progressivity; measures to improve tax assessment and collection; measures to improve export incentives (for example, exemptions or rebates of import duties, wage taxes, social security contributions)

SOURCE: Author.

TABLE 6.17   Main Characteristics of the 1953 Episode

Broad nature	most QRs, special import levies, and export subsidies abolished; 100 percent devaluation
Magnitude	large change; overnight change with no reversals for about three years
Stages and targets	none
Economic circumstances before liberalization	
Rate of real growth	less than 3 percent per annum
Rate of inflation	from 12.6 percent in 1951 to 5.1 percent in 1952
Agricultural production	5.6 percent decrease in 1952
Manufacturing production	1.6 percent decrease in 1952
Balance of payments	deficit greatly reduced
Balance of trade	deficit reduced
Severely restricted external trade	yes
Budget deficit	significant reduction of total budget deficit; surplus in ordinary budget
Dependence on external aid	yes
Accompanying policies	
Exchange rate	single, fixed
Export promotion	first, reduced by abolition of direct export subsidies; later, some indirect export subsidies introduced
Export duties	temporarily imposed on a few basic items
Monetary policy	expansion of M3 and lending; deceleration later
Fiscal policy	cautious; additional revenue needs due to earthquakes; ordinary budget shows surplus; growth of total budget deficit decelerated
Capital movement	inflow greatly encouraged
Economic performance	
Inflation	initial rise to 10–15 percent, subsequent reduction to 5.7–2.3 percent
Exchange rate	stable
Real wages	increased to 3.5–4.0 percent per annum in 1956
Employment	unclear; no data available; may have increased a bit
Real growth	accelerated; around 7 percent per annum
Protection	reduced considerably; increased a bit in 1955–56
Imports and exports	total trade increased substantially; trade deficit decreased, then increased

SOURCE: Author.

a regime of price transparency. The economy's development since the reforms underscores the beneficial effects of this change. The growth rate of GNP, the manufacturing sector, real wages, profitability, and capacity utilization were much higher after the trade liberalization than in the years preceding it, both on average and in trend.

Liberalization had an equally beneficial impact on the budget. The reasons for this effect were, first, the removal of the QRs and the related increase in the value of imports, which led to a large, real rise in customs revenues, and, second, the elimination of government outlays for direct export subsidies. In the record of rapid economic growth that followed the trade liberalization, it is not possible to identify sources of increased budgetary spending attributable to these reforms.

Similarly, the trade reform had no adverse impact on the balance of payments. On the contrary, the large rise in the dollar value of exports of goods and services and in net inflow of capital financed substantial increases in imports, which more than doubled in dollar terms between 1953 and 1957, and in foreign reserves, which were maintained throughout this period at a level of about four months' imports. This is a remarkable performance, considering that foreign aid, which had been substantial, came to an abrupt end in 1955. Foreign aid to Greece in 1952, for example, already on its descent, was US$182 million (down from its peak of US$263 million in 1950), or about 60 percent higher than the value of total merchandise exports of Greece.

The trade liberalization was sustained because of the prudent fiscal and monetary policy followed throughout the 1950s. It was the firm determination of all Greek governments of the 1950s to restore monetary stability by effectively reducing aggregate demand. Greek authorities felt that without such stability there would be no chance for the trade reforms to succeed, and they were bold enough to implement contractionary and trade-reform policies simultaneously.

Budgetary deficits from 1954 onward never exceeded in any year 2.7 percent of GNP. This conservative fiscal stance was complemented by careful monetary policies that succeeded in bringing the inflationary pressures of the early 1950s under control. By 1957 the annual rate of inflation had been reduced to 2.3 percent, as compared with rates of 12.6 percent in 1951 and 15.0 percent in 1954. Indeed, the trade reform of 1953 and its accompanying fiscal and monetary policies were responsible for a stable foreign sector for the next twenty years. In this period the real exchange rate remained firm, and the official rate set in 1953 was unchanged. Between 1953 and 1974, Greece's average, annual per capita income grew by about 7.0 percent, whereas the average rate of inflation was about 2.5 percent. This is indeed an exceptional performance, the foundation of which was set in April 1953.

Notes and Reference

Notes

This chapter is based almost entirely, with permission, on a study by George C. Kottis (1989). Professor Kottis's study is one of several prepared for the World Bank research project, "The Timing and Sequencing of a Trade Liberalization Policy." The conclusions reached in this chapter are entirely mine, however, and do not necessarily reflect the views of Professor Kottis or of the World Bank Group.

1. Since domestic industry did not produce technologically advanced equipment, these restrictions did not prevent the importation of such capital goods.

2. A superminister in charge of all sectoral and economic ministers.

Reference

Kottis, George C. 1989. *Liberalizing Foreign Trade: The Experience of Greece*. World Bank Comparative Studies. Washington, D.C.: World Bank.

CHAPTER SEVEN   GUILLERMO DE LA DEHESA

Spain: Trade Liberalization after 1959

In many ways, Spain's economy has performed rather successfully in the second half of the twentieth century. It is difficult to identify historical phases of economic growth in Spain as long as those that the country has enjoyed since 1950. Nor is it easy to find long periods of recession or sharp decreases in real GDP since 1950. In fact, from 1959 to the present real GDP declined in only four years: 1945, 1948, 1959, and 1981 (see Figure 7.1).

The evolution in the index of real GDP allows us to identify four main phases in recent Spanish economic history:

1. the import-substitution period covering the years from 1940 to 1959

2. the years of economic acceleration, 1960 to 1975

3. the period 1976–1985, when Spain's newly established democracy was forced by a decade of external shocks to adjust its economic system to the new international environment

4. the period since 1986, in which Spain joined the European Economic Community (EEC), initiating a period of high growth after four years of adjustment and of preparation for accession

The long phase of growth enjoyed by the Spanish economy would not have taken place without a parallel process of liberalization, reinforced

Figure 7.1   Long-Term Growth, 1941–1986

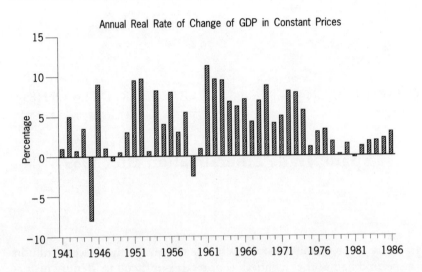

Annual Real Rate of Change of GDP in Constant Prices

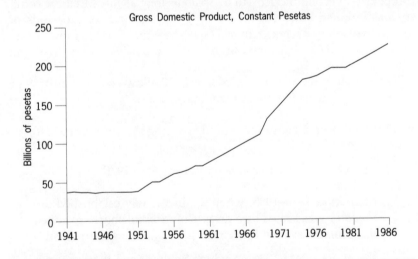

Gross Domestic Product, Constant Pesetas

SOURCE: de la Dehesa, Ruiz, and Torres 1990, fig. 1.1.

and accelerated by Spanish accession to the European Economic Community (see Figure 7.2). The four periods of growth identified in the preceding paragraph were largely made possible because major episodes of trade and economic liberalization set the productive forces of the Spanish economy free from regulation and intervention and exposed domestic production to foreign competition. These episodes were the 1959–1966

Figure 7.2   Trade-Liberalization Index, 1960–1986

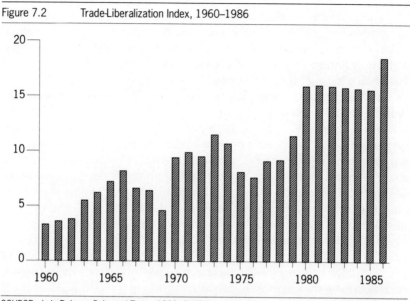

SOURCE: de la Dehesa, Ruiz, and Torres 1990, fig. 2.1.

episode initiated with the 1959 stabilization plan; the 1970–1975 episode that started with the 1970 Spain-EEC preferential agreement; the 1977–1980 episode that originated with the beginning of political democracy in Spain; and, finally, the 1986–1990 episode that was born with Spain's accession to the EEC.

The First Liberalization Episode, 1959–1966

Economic and political circumstances. The stabilization plan approved in July 1959 came in the middle of General Francisco Franco's dictatorship and, at the same time, during the most difficult economic situation the dictatorship had faced since the end of the Second World War.

Franco had developed an economic policy based on autarchy and import substitution. This policy was, in part, imposed by the international political blockade against the dictatorship, a blockade only partially broken by the military agreement with the United States in September 1953, in the depths of the cold war. Spain was isolated from the main political and economic developments in Europe and elsewhere; however, the course of economic policy also reflected an ideological choice. The underlying ideology of the Franco regime was a mixture of the traditional conservative values of the church and the army, and the economy was totally repressed in the name of politics.

This alliance of isolation and conservatism brought Spain to an economic dead end, with a highly overvalued exchange rate, a permanent balance-of-payments deficit, extremely low reserves of foreign currency, a rising inflation rate, and, of course, a small and inefficient industry based on a highly protected domestic market.

In these circumstances Franco's advisers—in particular his deputy, Admiral Carrero Blanco—convinced him to bring new blood into the government in 1957. The main argument was that the government needed to bring to power young economists and entrepreneurs who would maintain the regime's traditional values but who could bring some modernization to the regime and could try to derive some benefits from the European economic boom by breaking Spain's political and economic isolation. Despite these potential benefits, the opposition of Franco and some of his aides to this change was still great. The event that finally unleashed the stabilization plan was the report issued by the minister of commerce in July 1959, stating that the country was virtually bankrupt and could not make any payment in foreign currency, even for the most necessary imports of foodstuffs. The report said that the fees to join the World Bank and the IMF had been paid through a loan obtained from the Manufacturers Hanover Trust. It was the threat of insolvency contained in this message that finally made Franco change his mind.

The liberalization policy. The liberalization and stabilization program was contained in a memorandum sent by the Spanish authorities to the IMF and Organization for European Economic Cooperation (OEEC) in June 1959. In this document Spain's commitments to liberalization in the foreign sector were defined. The most important are summarized in the following paragraphs:

A system of uniform exchange rates was introduced, and practices giving rise to multiple exchange rates were abolished. In accordance with IMF guidelines, an initial par value of sixty pesetas per U.S. dollar was established, representing a substantial devaluation.

Spain agreed to liberalize very rapidly at least 50 percent of its imports with convertible currency countries (with 1950 as a base year). Nonliberalized private trade would be undertaken under a system of nondiscriminatory quotas, except for a margin of up to 10 percent that could be reserved for imports subject to individual licensing. State trading was to be limited almost exclusively to agricultural products. Imports with nonconvertible-currency countries would continue under bilateral trade and payment agreements.

On July 27, 1959, to avoid an unsustainable trade deficit and as a temporary measure to sterilize part of the money supply, the authorities began to require an advance deposit of 25 percent of the f.o.b. import value for all private imports. The requirement was suspended on January 23, 1960.

A tariff reform was announced. The general level of duties would be higher than before but not so high as to jeopardize import liberalization. The new tariff structure became effective on June 8, 1960.

A new foreign-investment law was passed, providing more incentives and facilities to attract foreign capital. The timetable of commitments for the second half of 1959 and for 1960 was in general fulfilled, with some minor delays of little significance. For the future, it is worth noting that, though the Spanish authorities stated their commitment to continue trade liberalization as long as the balance-of-payments position allowed it, no measurable end targets were fixed, no future stages were clearly contemplated, and it was not made explicit whether the intention was to accelerate or decelerate the process.

The Second Liberalization Episode, 1970–1975

The second liberalization attempt began in 1970 and ended in early 1975, when the government approved a number of decrees aimed at reversing the trade-liberalization experiment. The starting point was June 29, 1970. On that date Spain, after difficult negotiations with the EEC, finally signed a preferential agreement that became effective on October 1.

Economic and political circumstances. Around 1966 the expansionary cycle that started in 1960 began to lose momentum. The inflation rate was rising, and the balance-of-payments equilibrium was eroded in spite of an ever-growing net-services surplus. Faced with this situation, the economic authorities were forced to change their macroeconomic policies. In November 1976, an economic program was approved that included a devaluation of the peseta by 16.7 percent; tighter financial policies; and a freeze of prices, wages, and other incomes in 1968 and 1969. The program was very successful; the inflation rate plummeted, and the external account improved. All these results were compatible with a rather high rate of GDP growth. When the new liberalization was introduced, Spain seemed to have recovered macroeconomic stability. The economy in 1970 was growing at a rate above 4 percent, the inflation rate was slightly over 5.7 percent, and a current-account surplus was registered. Nevertheless, hidden beneath this economic stability lay several structural weaknesses and rigidities, in both the agricultural and the industrial sectors.

The liberalization policy. Two kinds of liberalization measures were undertaken, one derived from the EEC trade agreement and the other introduced later by the government. The EEC trade agreement included a clear timetable to ease quantitative restrictions (QRs) and to reduce nominal duties. Since only coal, iron and steel products, and commodities on the list of exceptions were excluded from the agreement, at least 60 percent of Spanish imports from the EEC were affected by tariff cuts.

The second component of this trade agreement was related to the QR system. The end target was to have only 5 percent of Spanish imports from the EEC under global-quota status by 1976.

The member countries of the EEC agreed to a substantial tariff reduction for Spain's industrial exports. The average tariff reduction amounted to 60 percent (30 percent in 1970, 50 percent in 1972, and 60 percent in 1973), although some exceptions were also contemplated. In agriculture, however, concessions were smaller, even lower than those granted to some other Mediterranean countries.

The Spanish government implemented a unilateral package of temporary liberalization measures between 1972 and 1974. After a selective reduction in November 1972, an across-the-board tariff cut for industrial products was introduced in June 1973. Goods were classified into three groups, depending on their degree of effective protection. Those with average and higher-than-average protection experienced nominal tariff cuts of 10 percent and 20 percent, respectively. Tariffs for goods with lower-than-average protection were not, in general, modified. For a small group of exceptional items, tariff reductions exceeded 20 percent.

In January 1974, a new linear reduction of 5 percent was applied on all goods except those with nominal tariffs under 5 percent; and this cut was extended to 10 percent in April 1974. In June 1975, however, when there was a deficit in the current account, the 1974 reductions and those introduced in 1973 were revoked.

Liberalization followed a similar pattern in easing QRs. QR abatement started in December 1972, when the Ministry of Commerce replaced the traditional exhaustive lists of liberalized products with a negative list; that is, all those goods that were not included in the list of restricted imports were automatically considered liberalized. Furthermore, in October 1972, June 1973, and June 1974, goods, both industrial and agricultural, that had been subject to state trading or quotas were placed under a free-import regime. This liberalization was reversed in October 1974 and February 1975, when all these goods again became subject to global quotas.

Through these policy reversals on tariffs and QRs, the degree of liberalization by mid-1975 became practically equal to that of 1966, except for the commitments within the EEC agreement, which were not reversed.

The Third Episode of Liberalization, 1977–1980

Economic and political circumstances. The third liberalization episode, between 1977 and 1980, consisted of an attempt at rapid liberalization, which slowed down when the second oil shock hit Spain's economy.

The main measures adopted were across-the-board and selective tariff cuts and some further easing of the QR system, as in the second episode, together with minor modifications in the government's export-promotion schemes (these schemes basically involved major provision of funds to support export credits and the mechanism of export-tax rebates).

Two international commitments helped to foster trade liberalization. On June 26, 1979, Spain signed a trade agreement with the remaining seven members[1] of the European Free Trade Association (EFTA). The agreement was designed to eliminate gradually all barriers to trade in industrial goods between Spain and the EFTA. The immediate effect of this agreement was that Spain extended to the EFTA countries the benefits accorded to the EEC members under the 1970 preferential trade agreement. The second international commitment derived from the consequences of the Tokyo Round of GATT negotiations. On July 4, 1980, Royal Decree 1323 approved the tariff reductions that were to be extended to GATT members.

The new liberalization attempt was launched by the first democratic government elected in Spain in forty years. There was a tremendous political shift in the government, and nearly all the public personalities of the Franco regime disappeared. Although Mr. Suarez, the prime minister, and other young ministers had been part of the later Franco cabinets, the political and social rules changed dramatically, and it was impossible for some people, mainly hard-line Francoists, to keep up with the new situation. The political force that won the 1977 elections, the Democratic Center Union (UCD), was a moderate political party constituted from a conglomerate of centrist and right-wing groups. It did not get an absolute majority in parliament and was forced to form some coalitions, mainly with the nationalist forces.

During the whole transitional period from the dictatorship to the consolidation of democracy, 1977–1983, the political structure was not perceived as stable. Terrorism and military unrest placed dramatic pressure on the newly established regime, as the 1981 attempted military coup clearly showed. Nevertheless, the government was certainly backed by all the major political and social forces in Spain. With this support it was able to develop its economic program, since all groups soon understood that the only way to secure democracy was to adjust the economic system to new international conditions and to integrate with Europe. Contrary to the second episode, the third episode included commercial policy as a major component of the economic program. Commercial policy was seen as an active contributor to improving the flexibility of the economy, enhancing the competitiveness of the tradable sector, and preparing the economy to join the EEC.

The liberalization policy. In this third liberalization episode there was no detailed program for implementing the projected reforms. Generalized transfers of commodities from the restrictive import regimes to a liberalized status started in January 1978 and continued in June 1978 and April 1979. Practically all goods that were subject to global quotas at the end of 1974 and the beginning of 1975 were again included in the free list, and other industrial and agricultural goods were also liberalized. From April 1979, there was no further progress in liberalization, except for specific items; and the structure of import regimes remained quite stable until March 1986. That date marked the start of the first stage of dismantling quantitative restrictions linked to Spanish integration into the EEC.

A temporary increase in tariffs and a 20 percent transitory surcharge, introduced in 1976, were abolished in February and July 1977. Tariff reductions begun in 1978 had the same transitory character as those in the second episode. In July 1978, the first three-month reduction was approved. It applied to industrial commodities and amounted to 20 percent on rates greater than 10 percent, although the reduction applied only to the portion exceeding 10 percent. A decree issued in April 1979 approved a new three-month across-the-board tariff reduction. Specific duties were lowered by 15 percent. Ad valorem duties underwent a concertina reduction, in which the overall range of charges was squeezed downward: rates between 0 and 10 percent were reduced by 10 percent, rates ranging from 10 to 20 percent were cut by 20 percent, tariffs between 20 and 30 percent were cut by 30 percent, and tariff reductions amounted to 40 percent for duties exceeding 30 percent. This decree was renewed in July, October, and January 1980.

In April 1980, the across-the-board reduction in ad valorem duties was modified. Rates of reduction were 18 percent for commodities taxed at tariff rates between 10 and 20 percent, 27 percent for rates between 20 and 30 percent, and 36 percent for rates exceeding 30 percent. These reductions were renewed periodically until March 1986, when new reductions linked to the EEC integration process were introduced. Additional reductions originating in the EFTA agreement and Tokyo Round became effective in July 1980.

The Fourth Liberalization Episode:
Spain's Accession to the EEC in 1986

Main characteristics. Accession to the EEC on January 1, 1986, initiated Spain's most important liberalization episode since 1959. The main characteristics of this new episode are described in the following paragraphs.

It is a multistage episode, programmed over a period of seven years ending December 1, 1992. By then Spain will be fully integrated into the EEC. Tariffs will be reduced to zero for goods coming from the EEC and the EFTA countries, and the common external tariff (CET) will be fully adopted for goods coming from the rest of the world.

It is a predetermined and an unmodifiable episode, since it was established by the Treaty of Accession and, therefore, was ratified by the parliaments of the twelve EEC members. The course set in 1986 cannot be reversed, since any alteration of the treaty will need the ratification of the twelve parliaments again. This makes any change practically impossible.

The episode is wider in scope than all the previous ones, since the liberalizing measures affect not only trade in goods and services but other current and capital movements, as well as fiscal and monetary policy and the institutional arrangements for most economic activities.

The liberalization commitments included in the treaty have been expanded in two important ways. First, autonomous initiatives have been taken by the Spanish government to liberalize further some areas not included in the treaty. Second, new liberalizing measures have been taken by the EEC in an effort to achieve a completely free common market by the end of 1992. These measures are included in the Single European Act, approved in 1986 by the European Council of Ministers and ratified by the twelve parliaments.

Liberalization measures included in the Treaty of Accession. All tariffs on industrial goods coming from the EEC and EFTA countries are to be reduced to zero over a period of seven years, according to the following timetable: March 1, 1986, 10 percent; January 1, 1987, 12.5 percent; January 1, 1988, 15 percent; January 1, 1989, 15 percent; January 1, 1990, 15 percent; January 1, 1991, 12.5 percent; January 1, 1992, 12.5 percent; January 1, 1993, 10 percent. The tariffs to be reduced are those that were effectively in force on January 1, 1985. This base was chosen to avoid any tariff manipulation during the negotiations. The same timetable of reductions is to be applied to all tariffs that exceed the CET for goods coming from third countries.

As of March 1, 1986, when the process started, all tariffs on industrial goods coming from Portugal and the developing-country members of the Lomé convention, as well as the preferential Mediterranean countries, were reduced to zero.

The treaty abolished all export tariffs; and all import and export licenses that were applied to trade with the EEC and EFTA countries, except for those applied to some agricultural products, were abolished.

Imports of cars from the EEC were made subject to a tariff quota with a reduced tariff of 17.4 percent (compared with the 1985 tariff of 36 percent) for a volume of 32,000 cars in the first year, 36,000 cars in the second year, and 40,000 cars in the third year. In the fourth year (1989), when the actual and the reduced tariffs coincided, the tariff quota disappeared. Imports of oil products and tobacco— traditionally restricted, since their distribution and production were subject to fiscal monopolies—also received tariff quotas with a yearly growth in volume and decline in rates.

Quantitative restrictions were drastically reduced (all data expressed at the four-digit level of disaggregation of the Brussels Tariff Nomenclature [BTN]):

- For industrial goods coming from the EEC the treaty allowed the survival of only 16 (of a previously existing total of 237) quantitative restrictions, including 4 for textiles, 2 for plastics, 4 for durable consumer goods, and 3 for arms and explosives. Forty-five other quantitative restrictions were permitted for reasons such as security, public order, or health. The first group of QRs was transitory and is set to disappear in seven years from the accession date, and the second group is permanent. The transitory QRs allow a yearly accumulated growth of 20 percent in volume or 25 percent in value.

- For agricultural goods coming from the EEC, QRs were reduced from 78 to only 26, 2 on a permanent basis and the rest on a transitory basis, to disappear during a transitional period of ten years.

- For goods imported from Portugal the reduction was almost the same: QRs on industrial goods were reduced from 237 to 45 and on agricultural goods from 78 to 37 (2 permanent and 35 transitory).

- For preferential countries (Mediterranean and the African, Caribbean, and Pacific countries associated with the EEC) the reduction was also substantial: from 237 to 62 (45 permanent) in industrial goods and from 78 to 56 (20 permanent) in agricultural produce.

- For GATT countries EEC Commission Regulation 288/82 allows Spain to maintain QRs that existed before it joined the EEC, provided both GATT and the commission are notified. Spain has also reduced QRs for goods imported from GATT countries from 238 to 89 for industrial goods (43 permanent) and from 97 to 53 for agricultural goods (14 permanent).

- QRs on Japanese imports have always been more important than those on other imports; but, in accordance with Regulation 288/82, Spain also reduced these QRs from 333 to 132 in industrial goods (47 permanent and 85 transitory) and from 97 to 53 for agricultural goods (14 permanent and 39 transitory).

- Finally, for state-trading countries a special EEC regime was prescribed in Regulation 1765/82 and Regulation 3420/83, which was more restrictive. Spain has adapted to such a regime, reducing QRs in industrial goods to 188 (of which 128 are permanent) if the country is a member of GATT and to 236 (of which 194 are permanent) if the country is not a member of GATT. For agricultural goods the reduction is to 57 (21 permanent) if the country is a member of GATT and to 54 (23 permanent) if it is not. These reductions in quantitative restrictions refer to QRs legally existing before and after Spain joined the EEC; but the number of binding QRs is lower, since many of them were not in use at the time Spain joined the EEC. The volume of all these QRs was based on the average value of imports in the period 1982–1985. The QRs are to grow at 12 percent per year in volume or 17 percent in ECUs (European Currency Units). If the use of a specific QR is less than 90 percent in two consecutive years, the QR is to be abolished.

Spain also agreed to grant developing countries access to its market under the generalized system of preferences.

Spain introduced a value-added tax (VAT) on January 1, 1986, following the policy to harmonize indirect taxes in all EEC countries. The introduction of the VAT and the elimination of the previous cascade tax (IGTE) also involved the abolition of the import tax (ICGI) and the export subsidy (DFE), which represented additional fiscal adjustments at the border. The IGTE, the ICGI, and the DFE (representing a 12 percent tax, on average) were very important in protecting imports and subsidizing exports; and their elimination has had a great impact on the performance of Spanish exports since the accession.

Macroeconomic performance. In 1986 Spain's economic performance was outstanding. Domestic product grew at 3.3 percent, whereas its average growth in the period 1980–1985 had been only 1.1 percent; private consumption grew at 4.2 percent, as compared with an average of only 0.4 percent in the preceding five years. Investment increased by 12 percent against 2.2 percent, on average, in the years 1980–1985. For the first time since 1977 net employment grew at a reasonable rate—about 2.4 percent, equivalent to 332,000 new jobs—whereas there had been an average annual fall of 227,000 in the preceding five years. In sum, 1986 was a positive year in macroeconomic terms.

The improvement in real income allowed not only an increase in consumption but also an increase in savings large enough to meet the demand for investment and to induce a current-account surplus that reached US$5 billion. The improvement in the current account was also no doubt due to the excellent performance of gross tourism receipts (US$12 billion) and to an improvement of around seventeen percentage points in the terms of trade. Foreign investment also set a record in 1986, reaching, in gross terms, US$8.2 billion, about 3.6 percent of GDP and 18 percent of gross capital formation. Finally, there was a net increase of about US$3 billion in reserves of foreign currency, despite a policy of foreign-debt repayment that reduced the stock of foreign currency by more than US$4 billion. At the end of December 1986 total foreign currency reserves accounted for US$17.3 billion and total foreign debt was US$24 billion.

In 1987, 1988, and 1989 macroeconomic performance was even better than in 1986. GDP growth was on average higher than in the first year of accession (5 percent), while employment creation was greater (3 percent), inflation lower (5 percent), and the public-sector borrowing requirement (PSBR) smaller (3 percent of GDP). The current account has gone into deficit, although foreign-currency reserves accumulated significantly, reaching US$45 billion, because of the increase in foreign investment (averaging US$10 billion a year in the period 1986–1989).

Concluding Observations

Spain's recent history provides a typical example of a long process of trade liberalization and growth. The smooth long-term tendency toward a more liberal trade regime was punctuated by three major upswings, in 1959 and 1960, in 1970 and 1971, and in 1977 and 1978—each followed by a short period of time during which liberalization did not progress—and by a final episode from 1986 until the present time, which has been determined by Spanish accession to the EEC. The core of the episodes has been tariff cuts, the loosening of the QR system, and the improvement of existing export-promotion schemes.

Common features of the liberalization episodes

International agreements. Each episode of this sustained process of liberalization has been supported by international influences, multilateral trade agreements, or international organizations, which have imposed, reinforced, or upheld the measures adopted by the economic authorities.

In the first liberalization episode, 1959–1966, the memorandum sent by the Spanish economic authorities to the OEEC and the IMF contained the core of the projected new strategy. Some rather clear targets were established, although the memorandum was ambiguous about the intention of the government to continue liberalizing in the years to come. The new strategy was successful; and, although it is difficult to quantify how closely results approached the targets set, it is commonly understood that liberalization went farther than anybody expected.

The second liberalization episode, 1970–1975, was guided by two different sets of policies. Although one of these was a package of unilateral measures, the first—and the one that initiated the episode—was the set of policies that followed the signing of the 1970 EEC preferential trade agreement.

The third liberalization episode, 1977–1980, shares some of the attributes of the second episode. There was no international agreement to initiate the episode officially, but the expectation of imminent integration into the EEC greatly influenced the decision to liberalize. Inflation concerns also played a role in the 1979 concertina operation.

The fourth liberalization episode is the one that shows the greatest influence of international obligations and demonstrates the usefulness of international agreements to consolidate trade liberalizations. The Spanish Treaty of Accession to the EEC, containing the most important liberalization measures ever taken for the Spanish economy, has been ratified by the parliaments of the twelve EEC members; and there is no possibility of reversal. I believe that Spain's long and sustained liberalization process has been made possible to a great extent by the existence of multilateral agreements and by international influences that have helped the liberalization tendency to continue. Liberalization attempts linked to multilateral agreements were always fully implemented and never reversed. Moreover—as is clear from the first, third, and fourth episodes—these external influences underwrote, directly and indirectly, the adoption of sound macroeconomic policies that allowed the unilateral liberalization measures to survive and helped the Spanish economy to become steadily more open (See Figure 7.3).

The level of reserves. The economic environment before the introduction of liberalization policies manifested some common conditions for the four liberalization episodes. Most people who determine economic

Figure 7.3   Openness of the Economy, 1964–1986

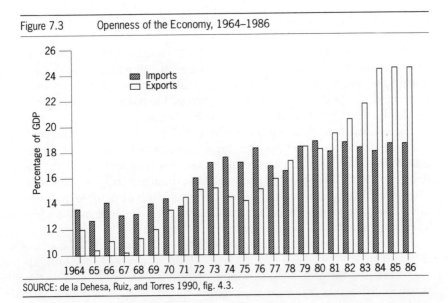

SOURCE: de la Dehesa, Ruiz, and Torres 1990, fig. 4.3.

policy in Spain believe in the existence of an "iron law" that has been positively tested throughout recent history. The law is, No economic reform can be implemented while the balance of payments is in surplus or equilibrium. The law could be more accurately stated as follows: The level of foreign-currency reserves has been the decisive factor in implementing all important economic reforms in Spain in the past fifty years. Unemployment or public-sector deficits have never been so important as the level of reserves.

As far as trade liberalization is concerned, our iron law is somewhat transformed and becomes, Only when the level of reserves is high enough and the balance of payments is in surplus or equilibrium is it possible to implement a trade liberalization in Spain (see Figure 7.4). There is no contradiction between these two versions of the iron law. In Spain "economic reform" has the same meaning as "economic adjustment," and the sequence of trade liberalization and economic adjustment that has prevailed in Spain's recent history reveals the following cycle: First the initial worsening of economic conditions unleashes the process of economic reform. "Bad economic conditions" usually means a low level of reserves caused by a bad balance-of-payments situation. Then comes the economic reform itself. It consists, in the first place, of a strong devaluation followed by fiscal and monetary tightening. Only when the balance of payments has recovered and the level of reserves has become sufficient is trade liberalized. After a few years of liberalization the external sector worsens, the orthodox policy mix is reversed,

Figure 7.4   Liberalization and the Current Account, 1960–1986

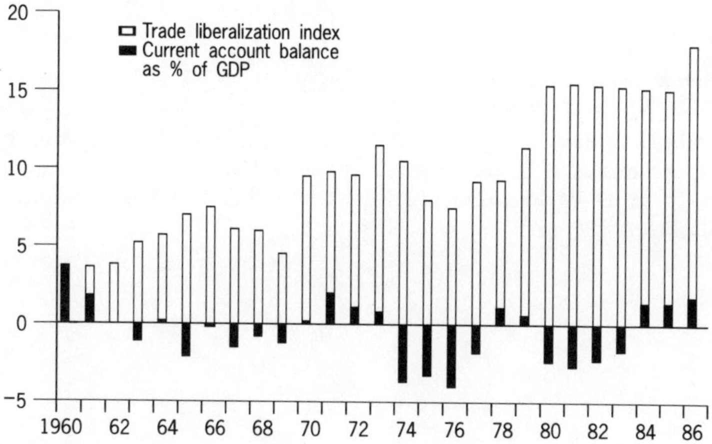

SOURCE: de la Dehesa, Ruiz, and Torres 1990, fig. 6.1.

and the whole process starts again. This is, in a very simplistic and rough way, what has been happening in the Spanish economy over the past forty years; but it cannot happen again after accession to the EEC, since there is no possibility of reversal.

In the same way, deceleration or reversal of liberalization policies has been associated with recurrent crises in the balance of payments. It is important to point out that in Spain there have been not total reversals but temporary interruptions in a long-term pattern of liberalization. Reversals or interruptions are now no longer possible, since the liberalization program has been agreed upon with the rest of the EEC and ratified by the parliaments of the twelve member countries.

In sum, economic liberalization in Spain has been a major source of steady growth and disinflation throughout the past thirty years of economic history, allowing Spain to be ranked today as one of the major industrialized countries of the EEC and the OECD.

Notes and Reference

Notes

This chapter is based on de la Dehesa, Ruiz, and Torres 1990.

1. Of the original nine, Great Britain and Denmark had dropped out to join the EEC.

Reference

de la Dehesa, Guillermo, José Juan Ruiz, and Angel Torres. 1990. "Spain." In *The Experience of New Zealand, Spain, and Turkey.* Vol. 6 in Liberalizing Foreign Trade, ed. D. Papageorgiou, M. Michaely, and A. M. Choksi. Oxford: Basil Blackwell.

CHAPTER EIGHT   OLI HAVRYLYSHYN

Yugoslavia: Trade Reform in a
Socialist Country, 1965–1975

Yugoslavia, like most developing countries, has conducted a more restrictive than liberal commercial policy in the past four decades. After
the political break with Moscow in 1948, however, Yugoslavia moved
toward the center of the political spectrum and turned westward in its
trade orientation. Trade policies then became gradually more liberal
and open; and in 1952 the first set of important reforms reduced the
state-trading monopoly and introduced an administered trade regime
with high protection, multiple exchange rates, and subsidy mechanisms
to promote selective exports of industrial goods. A major attempt to
liberalize the trade regime was made in the decade between 1965 and
1974; but it did not achieve its goals of currency convertibility, market-
based determination of prices, and improvement in Yugoslavia's international competitiveness. The liberalization was only partially
implemented before it began to be reversed in the late 1960s and early
1970s, so that by the end of the 1970s the trade regime was nearly as
restrictive as it had been before 1964.

The long-term evolution of trade policy in Yugoslavia is shown in
Table 8.1. Since 1952 the state-trading monopoly that typifies most socialist states began to be replaced with a more open and less restrictive
regime. Yugoslavia moved through a system of multiple exchange rates
in the 1950s[1] to a slightly more transparent tariff system with a unified
exchange rate in the early 1960s. This change set the stage for the one
major attempt at trade liberalization in the mid-1960s. The program was
never adequately implemented, however, and after about a decade of

TABLE 8.1	Evolution of Trade Policy, 1946–1986
1946–1952	State-trading monopoly
	Administered trade
	Multiple exchange rates
1952–1960	High protection and antiexport bias
	Tariffs and uniform exchange rate
1961–1964	Devaluation
	Major liberalization
	Lower tariffs
	Reduced import restrictions
1965–1974	Exports first liberalized
	Devaluation
	Decentralized ad hoc interventionism in trade
	Occasional devaluations
1975–1983	Increased tariffs and import restrictions
	Growth in export subsidies
	Stabilization program
	Planned reductions of import regulations and price controls
1986	Recentralized and reliberalized foreign exchange

SOURCE: Author.

back-and-forth movements the regime slipped back to a highly restrictive form. The only new factor was that the central government had
much less control of, and local and regional governments had increased
influence on, such things as prices, allocation of foreign exchange, export subsidies, and even import restrictions.

The availability of easy international credit removed the pressure to
earn one's import capacity through competitive export capability. Thus
the perceived importance of trade policy reform fell far into the back-
ground—until the debt crisis of the 1980s, when Yugoslavia, like many
other countries, was pressured by its external-imbalance problems to
readdress programs of trade liberalization. In Yugoslavia this renewed
attention to liberalization came in 1986 and was closely connected to
World Bank adjustment lending programs and support from the International Monetary Fund.

In Yugoslavia, then, the postwar trend has been one of gradual and
limited liberalization at first, followed by a more substantial effort between 1965 and 1975. This major effort did not succeed, and the regime
was allowed to retreat into considerable bureaucratic controls, nontariff restrictions on imports, and substantial government support to
promote exports on a selective basis. One small success eventually
achieved was institutionalization of regular exchange-rate adjustments
by means of a crawling peg, plus occasional further devaluations; but

this came only in the late 1970s. Why was the 1965–1975 liberalization effort reversed in Yugoslavia, and what lessons may be extracted from this experience?

The 1965 Reform

Despite the move from a state-trading monopoly in 1952, it was not until 1965 that Yugoslavia attempted significant liberalization. In several respects the 1965–1967 policies were a repetition of 1961 (see Table 8.1). The dinar was again devalued, IMF credits were obtained to help the adjustment, tariffs were reduced sharply to 10.5 percent, and the coverage of liberalized imports was increased. Liberalized imports accounted for 25 percent of value in 1965, 41 percent in 1966, and 36 percent in 1967. In addition to being much more far-reaching than in 1961, the 1965 liberalization measures also differed on the export side, since virtually all subsidies were abolished. Retention quotas of 7 percent were, however, maintained, as were other export supports, including selective fiscal and credit benefits.

The 1965 economic context also differed from that of 1961. Whereas the 1961 program was mostly a trade-policy reform, trade policies were only one aspect of the 1965 reforms, which are widely considered a major step in the evolution of the Yugoslav workers-management system of economic decision making. Although the basic mechanisms of such a system were established by 1952, the power of central planners remained dominant. According to the 1965 reforms, decisions were to be made increasingly by workers in factories, and domestic price setting was to be decontrolled and made more subject to market influence. Trade liberalization, although clearly consonant with the overall philosophy of the reforms, was only one element in them.

Although the steps taken in the years 1965–1967 were substantial, by 1968 they began to be reversed gradually. Some attempts in the early 1970s to reinvigorate the progress of liberalization were finally given up by 1974, when a major decentralization of power to self-management enterprises and local governments shifted control over foreign-exchange allocation, price setting, export credit and subsidies, and even import restrictions, away from the central government. Though this exercise in federalism by no means completely emasculated central power, it undermined it considerably and allowed local interests to dominate national objectives, balkanizing the trade-policy regime. This decentralization, however, was not the only or even predominant reason for the failure of liberalization, which had, after all, a decade in which to operate and become established. The reasons why the 1965 liberalization failed are described next.

Liberalization Reversed

There were two broad factors which led to the reversal and eventual failure of liberalization in Yugoslavia. The immediate faults were inappropriate macroeconomic and exchange-rate policies. The underlying long-term failures included persistence of distorted prices and incentives, which were never eliminated in the short-lived liberalization; the substitution of ad hoc and compensatory export-support programs for true import liberalization; and the deterioration of financial discipline at the microeconomic level as firms and local governments were given freedom to make decisions but were not held responsible for failures.

Before 1965 Yugoslavia had been one of the star performers in development, achieving rapid economic growth and considerable industrialization (see Table 8.2). Indeed, it outperformed most other newly industrialized countries in this period, even while maintaining extremely low inflation rates (1.5 percent annual). Since then it has seen continual deterioration in growth and, especially, in external competitiveness. The current-account balance, which had improved considerably between 1965 and 1970, deteriorated sharply to –2.4 percent in the 1970s; and this decline actually understates the worsening of competitiveness, since considerable earnings from tourism and remittances from guest workers in Europe filled a lot of the gap in the trade balance. This gap averaged –5 percent of GDP in the 1965–1970 period, largely because of the sharp deterioration in export performance, which fell to an annual 2.9 percent. As the last row of Table 8.2 shows, in the 1950s Yugoslav exports grew at 1.2 times the world average; but from 1965 through 1970 they slowed to be about equal to the world average (1.0), and in the 1970s were below the world average (.95), falling even farther below that average in the early 1980s.

One could not attribute this economic slowdown in Yugoslavia to the liberalization, for it is clear that the deterioration deepened after the liberalization was reversed in the 1970s. (The higher GDP growth was not gained through efficiency—see the declining incremental capital-output ratio [ICOR] and labor-productivity values of Table 8.2—but was bought through external debt, which financed continued high investment.) Furthermore, as was described above, the liberalization was limited and short lived, with reversals beginning as early as the 1968–69 fiscal year.

Errors of Macroeconomic Policy

The major reason for the economic slowdown in the early liberalization period was that the complementary macroeconomic policies were far

TABLE 8.2   Overview of Economic Growth, 1954–1985
             (annual growth rates or share)

	1954–1964	1965–1970	1973–1979	1980–1985
Growth in main aggregates (%)				
GDP	8.6	5.3	6.10	0.9
Gross fixed investment	9.2	5.3	8.00	−7.8
Total consumption	7.5	5.1	5.60	−0.9
Employment[a]	6.2	2.0	4.20	2.5
Exports of goods	11.9	8.2	2.90	4.0
Imports of goods	11.4	11.7	7.50	−7.5
Implicit GDP deflator	1.5	11.2	17.80	45.2
Share in GDP (%)				
Manufacturing (end year)	39.1	28.9	30.90	35.0
Investment (total)	33.0	38.1	42.20	38.1
Gross fixed investment	30.5	30.5	34.10	25.5
Changes in stocks	2.5	7.6	8.10	12.6
Domestic savings	29.5	37.0	39.80	38.5
Current-account balance	−3.0	−1.1	−2.40	−0.5
Factor price indicators				
Labor productivity[a]	5.4	3.8	1.80	−0.2
Net income per worker[a]	5.3	5.1	3.40	−6.7
Real interest rate on saving deposits (%)	—	−2.0	−9.60	−18.8
Maximum real lending rate (%)	—	−0.5	−7.80	−10.8
Efficiency indicators				
ICOR, industry	2.8	3.4	4.50	9.3
Ratio of Yugoslav export growth to world export growth	1.2	1.0	0.95	0.9

NOTE: Dash = not available.
a. In the social sector.
SOURCES: Federal Institute of Statistics, Yugoslavia, *Statistical Yearbook of Yugoslavia*, various issues; National Bank of Yugoslavia, *Quarterly Bulletin*, various issues; Dubey 1975; Havrylyshyn 1990.

too restrictive for the conditions of the economy. Though inflation pressures existed and were high by Yugoslav historical standards (over 10 percent), they were by no means critical. Monetary authorities reacted strongly also to the one-time "inflation" adjustment of decontrolled prices in 1965 (prices of some goods were adjusted by as much as 25 percent) and imposed severe monetary restraint, so that growth of the money supply fell from about 10 percent in 1964 to 4–5 percent in the next two years and –5 percent in 1967. As the economic downturn[2] frightened authorities, monetary policy overreacted in the other direction, with growth in the next four years averaging nearly 20 percent and fueling the very inflation it had earlier tried to contain.

Another major policy error was inadequate devaluation. The 1965 devaluation spurred early export growth; but the nominal rate was unchanged until 1971, whereas prices doubled in the interval. Failure to sustain depreciation of the real exchange rate undermined export performance and encouraged imports, which (at least until around 1969 and 1970) were less restricted than they had been before 1965. Deterioration of the trade balance, combined with slower growth of output and, especially, of industrial employment, engendered strong political pressure to reverse liberalization, since it was perceived to be taking away jobs. This perception is not consistent with the fact that in the first three years of liberalization (1965–1967) export growth (9.6 percent) exceeded import growth (7.4 percent), largely because of the sharp one-time devaluation in 1965. Indeed, as the liberalization measures were gradually reversed from 1968 on, import growth surpassed export growth despite the tightening of imports and foreign exchange allocation, because the real exchange rate was allowed to appreciate substantially.

What lessons may be found in the Yugoslav experience? First, it would be absolutely wrong to generalize from the Yugoslav experience and suggest liberalization of trade should be supported by expansionary macroeconomic policy. In the circumstances of Yugoslavia in 1965 this would have been appropriate only because there were few inflationary and deficit-financing pressures. Inflation rates were not extremely high, public budgets were generally balanced, and the only important imbalance was the external one. It was unnecessary to cut expenditures. With large public deficits and strong inflationary pressures, as seen in Yugoslavia today and in many Latin American economies, expansionary policy to help trade-liberalization adjustments is far too risky and is likely only to exacerbate the imbalances.

Indeed, the appropriate macroeconomic policy to complement trade liberalization is not country-specific but situation-specific. Consider present-day Yugoslavia. It now has an inflation rate over 100 percent and a large hidden public deficit (in the form of cumulated enterprise losses covered by unsustainable levels of interenterprise promissory-note credits). No adjustment of trade policies can ignore the need for stabilization in Yugoslavia.

A second lesson of the 1965–1975 reform is that it confirms the wisdom of regular adjustments of the nominal exchange rate, at least to match inflation—a lesson that Yugoslavia learned rather late. Furthermore, it is clear that the lack of real exchange-rate devaluation can undermine all the benefits of import liberalization—or, conversely, that devaluation can achieve a great deal in the short run, even if liberalization is limited, as it was in the first three years of the experiment in Yugoslavia.

Underlying Microeconomic Failures

The problems of firm-level indiscipline and of export-promotion strategies are the two most important microeconomic lessons of Yugoslav experience and will be elaborated in separate sections of this chapter. A number of other underlying problems in the Yugoslav experiment also merit comment. First is the question of the speed and degree of liberalization. Yugoslav liberalization was far more limited than either the economy or the polities could bear. This can be said despite the fact that there were strong demands for reversal by 1968. The will of the central authorities and the opportunity to undertake major adjustments of incentives was great in 1965, yet the steps taken were too limited to achieve the potential benefits of adjustment from import substitution to a more efficient export-based strategy. The positive results were also limited; and, in view of the macroeconomic policy, it is not surprising political pressures for reversal manifested themselves so quickly. Any credibility its actions had rapidly eroded as the government yielded to such pressures.

A related point concerns the loss of central influence over economic policy. The objectives of economic liberalization for firms coincided with the political need of the multiethnic Yugoslav federation to decentralize power; however, decentralization was carried too far. There was so much decentralization of government budgets that fiscal policy had little potential for effectiveness. This put all the onus for macromanagement on monetary policy, and this one tool was inadequate to the task of controlling inflation and stimulating the economy at the same time. Consequently, macromanagement seesawed from the highly restrictive to the highly inflationary.

In fact, control over monetary policy was also eventually lost through the decentralizing reforms, as local and regional banks began to issue new forms of money essentially supporting their local client enterprises' promissory notes to each other. The central authorities had the choice of allowing any excesses from this system to lead to bankruptcies or of propping up the system by conventional monetary issue of the central bank. Under pressure of threatened job losses and regional-interest lobbying they usually chose the latter. That is, they not only lost control of money-supply management but acquiesced in the inflationary expansion of money through the balkanized banking system. One result of this weakness is a new distinction of Yugoslavia: it was the only country in the world to attain triple-digit inflation in the 1980s, when the general global tendency was to reduce inflation. Another result of this accommodating policy is that it supported the financial indiscipline of firms, enhancing the soft-budget attitude, which is the subject of one main lesson from the Yugoslav experience.

The soft budget and adjustment to trade liberalization. Trade liberalization benefits an economy by allowing world prices to be reflected in domestic competition, which serves to guide resources into the most productive activities. Liberalization also stimulates increased productivity in reaction to external competition. The incentive of profits and the disincentive of losses by enterprises that do not restructure or increase productivity are the mechanisms that drive the adjustment. Anything that reduces the carrot of profits and the stick of losses will inhibit the working of this process. In Yugoslavia the evolution of a soft-budget environment did in fact become a major impediment to any attempt at adjustment.

The problem was not simply one of a typical socialist economy's lack of profit incentives. The system of self-management—even though incompletely applied in practice—did allow an enterprise both the freedom to operate on the market and the incentives to worker-owners of sharing fully in the profits made. The carrot was there but not the stick. Enterprises that did poorly were by law subject to closure and bankruptcy, just as in a capitalist economy; but in practice these steps were almost never taken. The number of jobs lost in liquidation procedures has always been minuscule in Yugoslavia. These losses reached a maximum of 8,000 in 1965 and, more typically, were about 2,000 annually—a tiny fraction of employment in the industrial sector of well over 1 million in this period. Instead, enterprises in difficulty have always been rescued by financial support, fiscal privileges, informal restriction of competing imports, or additional support for exported products.

The process of decentralization exacerbated this problem, since it gave more power to local and republic governments whose political interests were more closely tied to firms in their area than were those of the central government. It may be possible for the government in Belgrade to enforce closures of loss-making enterprises in Macedonia if it is doing the same for enterprises in Slovenia, Croatia, and elsewhere. It is politically far more difficult—and therefore less likely—for the Croatian government to stand by as a Croatian producer of electrical generation equipment is threatened by bankruptcy. Decentralization of economic power to the regions of this federalist state not only gave the local governments fiscal and other powers, it strongly encouraged them to use these powers to favor their region's firms against others. In the early years of liberalization this favoritism took the form of demands by the governments of the republics for rollbacks of liberalization to help firms supposedly affected by import competition. Later it included the use of control over prices; restrictions on local sales of goods, not only from outside Yugoslavia but even from outside the republic; and the use of the local government's revenue to help ailing firms.

Another important component of this soft-budget system was the new banking system established in 1965. Banks were no longer accountable to the central authorities as before, nor were they free to operate on the market for profit as in most market economies. Instead, they were to be founded and operated by a consortium of local firms and governments (republic and municipal). In effect, local banks were managed by their clients. Since real interest rates were negative throughout the period between 1965 and 1975 (see Table 8.2), this arrangement unsurprisingly gave easy access to credit for investment or working capital and provided little control of the financial viability of loans. As noted earlier, banks also provided the backup for a system of interenterprise credits in the form of promissory notes. Such credits had been a minor element in financing enterprise activities before 1965 (15–20 percent of liabilities). By the early 1970s this proportion had risen to 40 percent; and, though it fell somewhat in the late 1970s, it rose again sharply to 50 percent and more in the 1980s.

It soon became clear to the worker-managed firms that there was no significant penalty for financial problems and that a convenient mechanism existed through the interenterprise credit system and the local banks to fill the financing gap when expenditures exceeded income. Though the explicit use of government budget transfers was limited, the true extent of deficits was huge. This environment of financial indiscipline—known in Yugoslavia as the monopoly of the backward, in the literature of trade theory as rent seeking, and in public-finance theory as the problem of the moral hazard—undermined considerably any potential adjustment to a liberalized trade regime. When weak industries are given support because they need it, the incentive system of the economy takes on the perverse form of giving the greatest rewards to those that are least efficient.

The disincentives created by such soft-budget situations are not unique to Yugoslavia. An article in the *Wall Street Journal* (April 10, 1986, 32) describes this problem in Israel: "It appears that the best business strategy is to get into as much debt as possible and threaten to dismiss as many workers as possible. If you reach that happy state, ministers of every party will line up for the right to use taxpayers' money to keep you artificially alive." The inhibitive effect this support of weak enterprise has on economic restructuring is made explicit in another *Wall Street Journal* article (March 8, 1988, 30) headlined, "India's Other Sacred Cow, Sick Firms, Thwarts Gandhi's Economic Revolution."

The lesson in this discussion is simply that microeconomic incentives must be allowed to work reasonably well and that weak, loss-making enterprises cannot be indefinitely and without question rescued, for this will give the wrong message to all enterprises: that it does not pay to be efficient and to seek out the best profit-making opportunities.

TABLE 8.3	Export Subsidies as Percentage of Exports, 1957–1980		
1957	35.0[a]	1968	7.3
1960	15.0	1969	13.6
1962	24.0	1976	24.4
1964	45.0	1977	19.9
1964	20.0	1978	25.9
1965	20.6	1979	28.9
1966	6.3	1980	17.4
1967	4.4		

a. Industrial goods.
SOURCES: 1960, 1962, Sirc 1979, 24; 1964 (45%), Chittle 1977, 30; 1964 (20%), Dubey 1975, 38; 1965–1969, Mrkusic 1972, 43; 1976–1980, World Bank 1983, 79.

Instead of the dynamism needed in the process of adjustment, one will get instead complacency and inertia.

A review of export-promotion policies. The period of the administered trade regime in Yugoslavia (1952–1960) started with antiexport biases, but as the western orientation of the economy manifested itself, the need to earn foreign exchange led to changes favoring exports. These changes, however, did not consist of import liberalization aimed at reducing the bias favoring domestic production over exports; rather, the measures adopted were export-support mechanisms (subsidies, differential exchange rates) to compensate for the bias. Exports of heavy industrial goods benefited from a substantial subsidy of 35 percent (Table 8.3), whereas exports of agriculture, forestry, and services were effectively taxed between 16 and 21 percent. The incentives for consumer-goods industries were on the side of import substitution, with a protective effect of over 100 percent.

Export incentives continued to provide a proexport bias after the 1961 reforms. When a unified exchange rate was introduced, export premiums and subsidies reached levels as high as 45 percent in 1964. The devaluation of the dinar in general encouraged exports.

With the 1965 reforms, there was a sharp reorientation with the removal of most export subsidies. The initial effect of the 1965 liberalization was to begin simplifying the system and move toward neutral incentives by reducing both the import restrictions, which had produced an antiexport bias, and the existing export supports, which had served to compensate for this bias. The right beginning was made, but it was short lived. As the economic downturn led to a faltering of the will to liberalize, export subsidies were slowly reintroduced, tariffs that had been cut sharply were increased, nontariff restrictions on imports were also gradually increased, and ad hoc foreign-exchange allocation returned.

The antiexport bias developed further in the 1970s despite increased export subsidization. The lagging adjustment of the dinar; increased tariffs; increased nontariff protection of domestic industry through quotas, licenses, and foreign-exchange allocations; regional restrictions on sales; and price controls all combined to produce the strong antiexport bias typical of complex trade regimes. The best piece of evidence of this growing tendency toward antiexport bias since the mid-1960s is the export performance of Yugoslavia. As Table 8.2 shows, the pre-1965 period was one of rapidly growing exports, increased competitiveness, and controlled balance of payments. After 1965, the tendency reversed. Export growth slowed (though it was by no means low); world-market shares declined, especially after 1970; and balance-of-payments problems became a regular feature of the economy.

Why did the compensatory export-support policies that apparently worked so well before 1965 not work again in the 1970s? The simple answer is that the success of such policies as a substitute for true liberalization and neutrality of incentives is at best temporary and at worst illusory. These policies can help for a while to overcome import-substitution tendencies; but the effects are not sustainable in the long run if the complex structure of import restrictions remains in place. There are several reasons for this. First, the complexity of the system makes it difficult to know how much compensation is required for exporters to offset the bias. Second, exporters who depend on government assistance are as prone to inefficiency as those who produce for domestic markets under the shelter of import restrictions. Third, the arbitrariness of such systems leads to a policy of selected infant exporters picked not by the competitiveness of the global market but by government policy under the influence of existing interests.

In Yugoslavia, as in so many other developing countries, the infant-industry policies have favored exports of more capital-intensive and sophisticated goods over simpler labor-intensive goods. The Yugoslav pattern of evolution in manufactured exports is in stark contrast to that of South Korea (see Table 8.4). Starting with an emphasis on those goods in which it had a comparative advantage, such as textiles and clothing, South Korea within twenty years was exporting three times as much

TABLE 8.4	Yugoslavia and South Korea: Heavy and Light Goods as Percentage of Manufactured-Goods Exports, 1965 and 1985			
	Textiles and Clothing (%)		Machinery and Transport (%)	
	1965	1985	1965	1985
Yugoslavia	14	12	42	41
South Korea	46	27	5	35

SOURCE: World Bank 1987.

machinery and transport equipment as Yugoslavia. It is well known in American and European markets that Korea's Hyundai auto is a market buster, whereas Yugoslavia's Yugo is struggling to overcome an image of low quality.

One may say, however, that Yugoslavia has succeeded, after two decades of supporting infant industries, in achieving global competitiveness. Yes, to some extent this is true; but what matters is the cost at which success was achieved. In Yugoslavia, the export successes of ships, machines, electrical generation equipment, and transport equipment occurred early, at the heavy direct cost of export subsidization. Subsidizing these industries did not ensure continued improvements in efficiency to compete with new producers; therefore, these exports were sustainable in the 1970s only by more subsidization. The impact of this practice on firm and government deficits was covered over by heavy borrowing until the 1980s brought a halt to new credit. More important, the cost of export promotion by subsidy includes the indirect effect of lagging development in potential export industries in the labor-intensive consumer-goods categories, such as fresh and processed food for the neighboring European markets, textiles and clothing, footwear, and other consumer goods. In this sense the export-promotion strategy not only used the wrong tools (direct supports to exports) but fell into the common trap of promoting very advanced capital- intensive goods. The results were temporarily positive but ultimately illusory, since most of these goods did not have deep-rooted capacity to compete on world markets without such supports. These export supports were not in the long run able to substitute in Yugoslavia for a fuller across-the-board liberalization of imports, which is the only sustainable form of export promotion.

Notes and References

Notes

This chapter is based on Havrylyshyn 1990.

1. It is important, however, to bear in mind a unique institutional aspect of the Yugoslav economy. The system of multiple exchange rates was far more complex than such systems elsewhere. It comprised not only differences in the official exchange rate by type of transaction but also a centrally controlled price system, in which differences between domestic and world prices for particular goods traded were the basis for either subsidies from government to producer or retention of positive margins by the government.

2. GDP growth fell to about 4 percent in the years 1966–1968, and industrial employment actually declined by 3 or 4 percent.

References

Chittle, Charles R. 1977. *Industrialization and Manufactured Export Expansion in a Worker-Managed Economy: The Yugoslav Experience*. Tübingen: J. C. B. Mohr (Paul Siebeck).

Dubey, Vinod. 1975. *Yugoslavia: Development with Decentralization*. Baltimore: The Johns Hopkins University Press for the World Bank.

Havrylyshyn, Oli. 1990. "Yugoslavia." In *The Experience of Israel and Yugoslavia*. Vol. 3 in Liberalizing Foreign Trade, ed. D. Papageorgiou, M. Michaely, and A. M. Choksi. Oxford: Basil Blackwell.

Mrkusic, Zarko. 1972. *Teorijska Osnova Deviznog Sistema*. Belgrade: Institut Ekonomskih Nauka.

Sirc, Ljubo. 1979. *The Yugoslav Economy under Self-Management*. New York: St. Martin's Press.

World Bank 1983. *Yugoslavia Adjustment Policies and Development Perspectives*. A World Bank Country Study. Washington, D.C.

———. 1987. *World Development Report*. New York: Oxford University Press.

East Asia: Trade Reform in Korea and Singapore

South Korea and Singapore are two of the dramatic success stories of the past quarter century, and the rough outlines of their success are well known. Government intervention has been heavy in both countries, as it has been in Taiwan—but not in another East Asian success, Hong Kong. In both countries, however, as in Taiwan and Hong Kong, governments have constrained their own actions by their determination to be competitive on world markets. Consequently, the economic management of the countries has continually been subject to the test of the world market, much as firms in competitive markets are continually tested by those markets. The world market has quickly revealed mistakes in economic management and the aim of integration has required quick correction of these mistakes. In pursuit of their overall aim, both countries have retained enough flexibility in their economic management to make these corrections.

Republic of Korea

It is sometimes difficult to recall how bad the economic situation appeared in South Korea in the late 1950s. Per capita income was US$180 in 1960, and the general assessment of the country's prospects was negative. It was a war-divided ex-colony, with few physical resources. Yet by 1985 per capita income had risen to US$2,150. In 1960 exports were US$30 million; in 1985 they were US$30 billion.

The common perception of South Korea is of a country that has restricted imports severely and promoted exports vigorously. This view needs to be examined rather closely. In fact there have been three phases in Korea's industrial and trade stance since 1960. The first phase began with a change, in the early 1960s, from an inward-oriented, import-substitution policy stance to export promotion and a commitment to compete on world markets. At that time a multiplicity of export incentives was introduced, many of them aimed at enabling exporters to obtain imported inputs at world market prices (Kim 1990, 25; Hong 1979, 54–55). To a large extent the export incentives were available to all export industries; the government provided a general incentive structure for exports and did not attempt to select winners. A unified and realistic exchange rate was implemented through a major devaluation, interest rates were allowed to rise, and imports were significantly liberalized. The essence of the change, however, was to orient and to a large extent subjugate the whole policy structure to export facilitation and promotion.

The second phase started in 1973 with the reduction of export incentives, some of which overcompensated for import barriers on inputs into exporting industries, and, more importantly, with the inauguration of a policy to promote heavy and chemical industries. Several selective forms of protection for these industries were introduced. Although some of these industries have prospered, others have not; and the successes were achieved at high cost. (World Bank 1987a, chap. 2) The third phase came as the costs of the selective, key-industry approach were being realized. This phase involved reversion to a nonselective approach to industry promotion and a gradual reduction in barriers to imports, accompanied by a further reduction of promotion measures. If labels are to be applied, the first phase could be termed "mercantilist," the second "strategic industrial policy," and the third "liberalization"; but these labels simplify too much. Overall there has been a commitment to compete in export markets, and policy has mostly been aimed at removing the domestic obstacles to this competition.

As part of the World Bank's study on the timing and sequencing of trade liberalization, an index of liberalization has been constructed. It is reproduced as Figure 9.1. It can be seen that the author, Kwang Suk Kim, identifies two liberalization phases, separated by a decade in which the net effect of trade policy changes was neutral. In 1967 a change occurred that is not easily described in terms of overall measures. This change was a move from a positive list of import restrictions to a negative list, that is, a change from a list of allowable imports, all others being banned, to a list of restricted imports, all others being permitted without restriction. Although at any moment the two lists could be constructed to give identical results, the latter system, by shifting the onus, is in the

FIGURE 9.1   Korea: Index of Trade Liberalization, 1955–1984

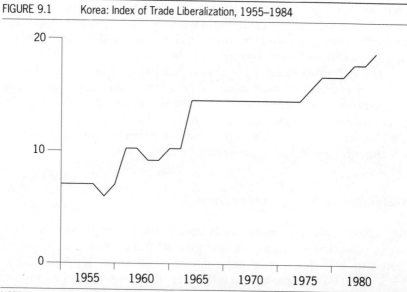

NOTE: The index ranges from 0 (no trade) to 20 (free trade). Points between 0 and 20 are the source author's judgment of the restrictiveness of the trade regime.
SOURCE: Kim 1990, fig. 3.1.

longer term a much more liberal and transparent policy instrument. In fact the change to the negative list had major immediate, as well as longer-run, liberalizing effects, since it was accompanied by a reduction in the coverage of import quotas (Kim 1990, 30, t. 3.3).

The year 1978 saw a deliberate change in policy stance directed toward opening the economy, marked by the establishment of an import liberalization committee. Since then the liberalization has been gradual, preannounced and steady, apart from a break in 1980, a year of severe recession. Only 50 percent of about 1,000 categories of imports were unrestricted in 1978; but by 1987, 95 percent of almost 8,000 import classifications were unrestricted (granted "automatic approval") (Kim 1990, t. 3.3; World Bank 1987a, t. 3.3). Apart from agriculture, priority for liberalization was given to highly protected sectors and to industries with monopolistic market structures, many of these industries having been encouraged during the 1970s. Of the 5 percent of import categories still restricted in 1988, three-quarters were primary products, for which protection has been increasing rather than decreasing over the past twenty or so years (Anderson and Hayami 1986, t. A1.2). Quantitative barriers are now effectively absent for the great bulk of Korean imports.

Since 1978 import tariffs as well as nontariff barriers have been reduced; but because of the number of tariff exemptions and drawbacks that previously existed for exporters, it is more difficult to determine the course of average operative tariff levels than to trace changes in quantitative barriers (Nam 1986, t. 2; World Bank 1987a, 68–73). The dispersion of tariffs is being reduced substantially, however; and this is an important element in reducing the costs of protection.

The shift from quantitative import restrictions and the reduction of tariff concessions have both made for greater transparency in the system of protection, and this in itself has reduced the costs of protection. Explicit financial assistance for exports has also been reduced so that since 1982 preferential interest rates have no longer been available to exporters, though they still have preferential access to loans.

Features of the Korean trade system

Big exports imply big imports. Much attention has been given to the very high proportion of gross domestic product (GDP) that is exported by Korea: in 1985 this was 36 percent, compared with only 9 percent in 1965.[1] What is often overlooked is that over the past decade or so imports have been a similar proportion of total expenditures. Unless a country has substantial aid or capital inflow, this must be so—the overall balance of payments must balance. (In fact, because of aid and capital inflow, in the years from the end of the Korean War until the early 1970s Korea's imports were a significantly greater proportion of its GDP than were its exports.) In order to import a country must export. The other side of this coin is that in restricting its imports a country also restricts its exports. Despite the significant control of imports that has existed, imports made up more than a third of gross domestic product from 1974 on, rising to as much as 44 percent in 1981 (World Bank 1984, t. A3.1; 1987a, t. A3.1).

The composition of the imports between 1975 and 1983 was 17–24 percent raw materials for use in exports, 23–34 percent capital goods, and 15–25 percent crude oil; the remaining 30–36 percent comprised all other imports. (World Bank 1984, t. 3.4). Of course much of the capital equipment and oil were also intended for the production of export goods—one estimate is that raw material imports for direct use in exports were about 25–30 percent of total imports in the first half of the 1970s and constituted 40–50 percent of exports (Hong 1979, t. 3.8). These are high proportions, but imports were not just inputs into exports. The basic point here is that a country cannot have an open economy on the side of exports and a closed economy on the side of imports. If a country wishes to export it must import.

Import restraints balanced by export incentives. In assessing whether the production incentives in an economy are biased toward self-sufficiency or toward exporting, estimates are made of the extent to which import barriers, which provide incentives for home-market production, are counterbalanced by incentives to export. Some incentives cannot readily be quantified; on the side of imports some forms of nontariff barriers to imports are particularly difficult to bring into quantifiable tariff-equivalent terms. On the side of exports, a national ethos of commitment to compete on world markets cannot be converted into a quantifiable export subsidy. Subject to these limitations, columns 2 and 3 of Table 9.1 present estimates of effective rates of exchange for imports and for exports. These figures measure the costs of imports and the returns from exporting after taking into account actual exchange rates and all

TABLE 9.1	Korea: Exchange Rates and Index of Competitiveness, 1962–1983				
	Official exchange rate (R.O.K. won to U.S. dollar)	Effective exchange rate (R.O.K. won to U.S. dollar)		Ratio of imports rate to exports rate (x100)	Competitive-ness indexc (1965 = 100)
		Exports[a]	Imports[b]		
	(1)	(2)	(3)	(4)	(5)
1962	130.00	141.8	146.4	103	85
1963	130.00	177.6	148.2	83	71
1964	214.31	263.6	247.0	94	88
1965	265.40	275.3	293.1	106	100
1966	271.30	283.8	296.4	104	97
1967	270.70	290.7	296.2	102	91
1968	276.60	294.8	302.5	103	88
1969	288.20	306.6	312.7	102	88
1970	310.70	331.5	336.4	101	91
1971	347.70	370.5	369.5	100	95
1972	391.80	404.3	415.2	103	104
1973	398.30	407.0	417.7	103	121
1974	407.00	415.6	425.5	102	105
1975	484.00	495.9	508.9	102	103
1976	484.00	496.3	515.4	104	97
1977	484.00	493.4	519.7	105	97
1978	484.00	495.0	526.9	106	102
1979	484.00	495.0	520.0	105	92
1980	618.50	639.1	652.9	102	96
1981	686.00	701.0	720.1	103	94
1982	737.70	740.7	779.5	105	91
1983	781.20	781.2	837.1	107	102

a. Official exchange rate plus net export subsidies.
b. Official exchange rate plus actual tariffs and tariff equivalents.
c. Official exchange rate adjusted for changes in the wholesale price index of Korea relative to those in the United States and Japan. The indexes of the United States and Japan are weighted by the average shares of those countries in Korea's total trade. An increase in this index implies real devaluation by Korea.
SOURCE: Kim 1990, t. 2.10.

measurable taxes and subsidies on both imports and exports.[2] The relation between the figures in columns 2 and 3, which is shown in column 4 of Table 9.1, shows the net relative incentive for import-substituting production against production for export. An index of more than 100 indicates net bias toward producing import substitutes rather than exports; a figure of less than 100 indicates a net stimulus toward exports. Many developing countries have had indexes of the order of 150 or more. It is rare for a country to register a figure lower than 100. Despite all the export-promotion activities in Korea, it seems that, in the aggregate, the measurable incentives largely offset, but did no more than offset, the barriers to imports. This general relationship has continued over the past decade as both the export incentives and the import barriers have been reduced. What is significant, however, is how close to 100 the Korean figure remains, so that there was not, as in so many other developing countries, a dominant overall incentive toward import substitution.

Korea has not had free, or almost free, trade or uniform barriers to imports; so there is a wide range of degrees of protection for various types of products. Protection against imports of agricultural products and transport equipment (including motor vehicles) has been particularly high. One way to show the overall effect of this nonuniform protection is to group products according to the extent to which they are directed toward the export or the domestic market. Table 9.2 presents such a classification and gives estimates, for each category, of effective protection against imports and of effective subsidies for exports.[3] Data for Singapore and Argentina are included for comparison. Argentina, it can be seen, effectively taxed all forms of exports. Korea effectively taxed some traditional exports (for example, ginseng) but effectively subsidized, to a moderate degree, exports in all other categories. Korea provided moderate negative effective protection on the domestic market, and positive export subsidies, to industries manufacturing goods for export—in marked contrast to Argentina, which heavily protected the domestic market and effectively taxed exports, even of those industries that exported most of their output. Those Korean manufacturing industries that did face significant competition on the home market were (on average, in 1968) protected on that market and also had significant assistance to export.

In summary, although in the aggregate Korea's incentives to export balanced the barriers to imports, the situation differed significantly according to product. Primary products aside, these differences between products have decreased significantly in recent years.

Nondiscrimination among exports. A notable feature of Korea's export assistance over most of the period since 1962 has been that the majority of its forms were available to all industries, not just to selected industries. (However, since much of the export assistance until the 1980s involved very favorable treatment of imported inputs, the effect could differ between industries according to the extent to which they used imports. This difference is reflected in Table 9.2.) Export promotion was not

TABLE 9.2   Korea (1968), Singapore (1967), Argentina (1969): Effective Rates of Protection against Imports and Effective Export Subsidies (percentages)

Industry	Korea		Singapore		Argentina	
	Protection against imports	Export subsidies	Protection against imports	Export subsidies	Protection against imports	Export subsidies
Export industries[a]	−26	9	8	6	−9	−14
Traditional	−90	−11			−12	−12
Nontraditional	−15	14	8	6	40	−26
Primary	−55	−5	13	13	−10	−14
Traditional	−90	−11			−12	−12
Nontraditional	−19	4	13	13	37	−29
Manufacturing	−15	16	−1	−1	71	−20
Export-and-import-competing industries[b]	52	8	9	−2	112	−32
Primary	17	3	15	−3	76	−10
Manufacturing	55	9	6	−1	120	−44
Import-competing industries[c]	83	31	15	−3	130	−59
Primary	72	2	72	0	32	0
Manufacturing	100	39	−1	−4	131	−59
Non-import-competing industries[d]	4	7	−6	−3	107	−40
Primary	8	9	−6	−3	46	−62
Manufacturing	−14	2	−6	−3	111	−42
All industries	10	9	1	8	55	−17
Traditional	−90	−11			−12	−13
Nontraditional	11	12	8	1	99	−33
Primary	11	0	15	4	4	−15
Traditional	−90	−11			−12	−13
Nontraditional	13	7	15	4	48	−44
Manufacturing	7	14	4	−1	116	−29

NOTES: Blank cell = not applicable.
Apart from the export industries category, which comprises traditional as well as nontraditional activities, all productive activities have been classified as nontraditional.
Effective Rates of Protection have been calculated by the Balassa method.
a. More than 10 percent of production exported, less than 10 percent of consumption imported.
b. More than 10 percent of production exported, more than 10 percent of consumption imported.
c. Less than 10 percent of production exported, more than 10 percent of consumption imported.
d. Less than 10 percent of production exported, less than 10 percent of consumption imported.
SOURCE: Balassa et al. 1982, t. 2.5.

generally operated with the intention of discriminating among export industries (Hong 1979, 68). The most significant departure from this policy came with the development of the heavy- and chemical-industry (HCI) program, started in the mid-1970s. Then it was that the government itself actually started to select particular industries for promotion, not for exports as such, though it was anticipated that a large part of the output would be exported. "Instead of following the lead of private enterprises in sectoral resource allocation, the government has tried to lead the entrepreneurs according to the expected changes in the Korean comparative advantage" (Hong 1979, 69). Not all of this leadership was successful in outcome, and success was even less in cost/benefit terms. Some of the industries selected contributed to the severe structural problems that Korea experienced from 1979 through 1981.

The Korean government's industrial policy of the 1980s turned back to setting the general policy environment rather than attempting to pick winners. This change

> stems in good measure from the HCI program which substituted bureaucratic judgment for market tests, was costly, and left scars on the economy in terms of distorted credit markets, overly-indebted firms, and a very high concentration of industrial power. [Further,] contrary to the preferentially financed huge capital investments of the HCI push, Government does not intend to be the risk partner for the country's emerging industries, such as electronics. (World Bank 1987a, paras. 13, 18)

Commitment to the world market. The commitment to compete on world markets has been important, not only in itself, but more particularly for the constraints it has imposed on other policies. From 1962 President Park chaired monthly meetings of senior economic officials together with directors of financial institutions and business associations, the presidents of leading export firms and trade associations, and experts on trade.

> Not only [do] the Korean exporters always get the immediate and close attention of the president, but the successful ones are regularly honored with honor medals. As a result, anyone who has accumulated wealth via export activities is almost considered a patriot and he is assured that he has the blessing of the government. This has an immense psychological impact in a society which still carries remnants of traditional Confucianism. (Hong 1979, 58)

Such attitudes and commitment are not easily transferred to other societies—indeed it is difficult to say how they develop in any society.

Nevertheless, commitment to an external constraint can be a most useful anchor to hold fast against those who seek the promotion of their own interests. Membership of the General Agreement on Tariffs and Trade (GATT) and the International Monetary Fund can provide support for programs of liberalization and have done so in Korea, as has pressure from the United States. A comparison is sometimes made in terms of Ulysses and the sirens: commitment to an external constraint, like being tied to the mast, can be useful in resisting those with special and seductive interests, but only if the rope is strong. The Korean commitment was credible, and in the two liberalization episodes in Korea (1965–1968 and 1979–) there was "no question but that the two trade liberalization programs would be implemented as announced by the government" (Kim 1990, 55). External constraints or anchors can strengthen the strong, but they may not be credible for others. As for Ulysses, the secret appears to be to take the action at a time of relative strength.

A trade stance supported by fiscal rectitude. Although the latter half of the 1970s saw quite rapid inflation in Korea, reaching 32 percent per annum in 1980, generally a tight rein was kept on fiscal deficits and monetary expansion. Starting in 1964 the government adopted a balanced-budget policy; from that time the budget deficit usually has been confined to 1 or 2 percent of GDP, with occasional surpluses. Although it reached more than 4 percent of GDP in 1982 (World Bank 1984, t. A6.1) the balance was turned around to a surplus of 1 percent in the following year. This financial prudence is reflected in the absence of any great worry about the external debt of Korea, despite its being (in 1985) 43 percent of GDP, with a debt-service ratio of 22 percent of exports. Such prudence appears to be the sine qua non of integration into the world market; genuine determination to integrate successfully into the world market itself constrains fiscal follies.

Realistic exchange rates. This point is closely related to the previous one, for it is much easier to maintain a realistic exchange rate, and reasonable stability in the real exchange rate, when inflation is moderate. Table 9.1 shows not only that the effective exchange rate for exports was kept close to that for imports, which itself reflects that the official exchange rate was realistic in terms of the market, but also that the index of competitiveness was quite steady. Because the exchange rate was adjusted to compensate for changes in relative price levels there was, with the exception of 1973 (under the influence of the OPEC price increase), no major shift in the index of competitiveness. Such a policy provides the basis for industry to plan, in the knowledge that what looks profitable today will not be rendered unprofitable by large nominal or real exchange-rate movements tomorrow.

The Korean government has been in no hurry to liberalize capital flows ahead of trade liberalization; and, in view of other policies, this approach has probably helped to bring real-exchange-rate and monetary stability. Much has been written on the question of the appropriate sequencing of trade and capital-flow liberalization, and the Korean experience does appear to give some support to the argument that trade liberalization should precede liberalization of international capital flows. It might also be noted that the domestic capital market in Korea is controlled and that external capital liberalization in such circumstances can bring problems.

Flexible reactions to external and internal shocks. The overriding objective of meeting the demands of international markets has required rapid and flexible reactions to internal and external shocks. Along with other countries, Korea was hit heavily by the oil-price increases of 1973 and 1974, experiencing a decline in its terms of trade of 23 percent relative to 1972. The real exchange rate was devalued, domestic energy prices were increased, exports were promoted, and loans were raised abroad (Krueger 1987, 192). Per capita GNP growth slowed to 6 percent in 1974 and 5 percent in 1975, climbing back to 13 percent in 1976 (Kim 1990, t. 2.1).

As were other countries, again, Korea was buffeted by increases in oil prices and interest rates and by international recession over the years 1979–1981. At the same time it suffered high inflation (19 and 32 percent in 1979 and 1980 respectively), poor harvests, and the assassination of President Park. In addition, it had earlier embarked on the costly heavy- and chemical-industry promotion, which many observers regard as being at best overdone, if not an error. Again, the correction was quick, orthodox, and successful. In 1980 real GNP per capita fell by 7.7 percent; within two years it had passed its previous peak. The 1980 inflation rate of 32 percent was halved in the following year, and in 1982 and 1983 it was 5 percent and 2 percent respectively (Kim 1990, t. 2.5, t. 5.1). Trade liberalization, which was interrupted in 1980, was resumed in 1982.

Singapore

Singapore is a city-state of 2.6 million people. In terms of population it is comparable to New Zealand, Nicaragua, Jamaica, and Uruguay, among other nations; but in terms of area, Hong Kong and Mauritius are among the few economies that compare.

It is sometimes suggested that a city-state has no option but to adopt an export-oriented trade strategy. If this is a matter of population, then there are many countries of similar size that have not followed this path. If it is a matter of land area, scarcity of food and raw materials may provide an imperative to trade; but apart from this possibility there seems to be little reason that does not also apply to other countries. So it would not be correct to assume that Singapore, which has integrated into the world economy and has freer international trade than almost any other country, had no alternative and that therefore there are no lessons for other, larger countries to learn from its experience. A growth rate for real per capita income of 7.6 percent for 20 years, to give an average income level of US$7,420 in 1985, in a country with few natural resources except a harbor and location, suggests that some lessons are available.

Singapore started on a path of import substitution. Having become independent from Britain in 1959, it was part of the Federation of Malaysia from 1963 to 1965 and for four years (1961–1964) pursued a policy of import substitution in the usual forms of import tariffs and quotas. When Singapore left the federation, import tariffs were increased, but often as import quotas were being removed. The real export orientation began in 1967, with the exemption of 90 percent of export profits from taxes and with other forms of export promotion, particularly for "pioneer" industries (Aw 1990, 27). As Table 9.2 shows, even in 1967 both barriers to imports and incentives to export were small when compared with those of other countries, except for the minuscule primary-industry sector. Import tariffs were raised to replace import quotas initially, so as to cushion the shock; but all tariffs and quantitative restrictions were known to be temporary and were reviewed frequently. Liberalization continued to 1973; by then all import quotas had been removed, and Singapore had returned to virtually free trade. The industrial structure was, however, still affected by considerable government guidance and encouragement, always subject to the constraint of world competition.

What is significant is how quickly Singapore abandoned the inward-orientation path and how committed it has been to competing on the world market since then. It is one of the few countries to have started and then stopped car assembly. All protection for this activity was removed by 1980. Also significant is the manner in which the government tamed the union movement so that it provided little opposition inside or outside parliament. Foreign investment has been encouraged throughout independence, and financial liberalization was regarded as a prerequisite for Singapore's successful development as an international financial center.

Many of the points made about Korea also apply to Singapore. As in Korea, the constraints of the international market have required fiscal discipline; and the Singapore government has continually run a substantial surplus on its current budget, with which it has financed, in a prudent manner, development expenditure. It has adjusted rapidly and in orthodox fashion to substantial dislocations from changes in oil prices. Like any other government, it has made some policy mistakes—an attempt was made in the early 1980s to induce an increase in productivity by pushing up wages ahead of productivity. The impact of this policy on the real exchange rate, trade, and growth brought an immediate signal that the policy had to be corrected to maintain the openness of the economy. Part of the solution was exported, in the form of reduced employment of Malaysians.

Singapore provides an excellent example of a country in which there is a great deal of government intervention in the domestic economy but in which, because of the openness of the economy, this intervention is continually subjected to a market test. The commitment to compete has been even greater in Singapore than in Korea, for virtually all industries producing tradable goods are exposed to foreign competition on the domestic market as well as on the export market.

A Note on Countervailing Duties

In both Korea and Singapore export-promoting subsidies were a part of the early drive into world markets, but in both cases these subsidies have been decreased over time. There are now no such subsidies in Singapore; in Korea preferential access to short-term loans remains as the only form. The current enthusiasm of the United States in particular for taking countervailing action against export-promoting subsidies, even when these subsidies are designed to offset a bias toward producing for the home market, makes the use of such subsidies less feasible now. It should be noted, however, that exemptions from import duties on imported inputs into exports are not regarded as subsidies.

For countries that wish to promote exports, the way is still open to remove the obstacles to exporting directly, rather than by attempting to compensate for these obstacles by providing subsidies. In large part the obstacles to exporting by most countries are provided by restrictions on imports, not in foreign countries, but in the countries that are attempting to export. As stated earlier, a country that shuts out imports locks in its exports. Removing obstacles to importing provides a more efficient way to promote exports than does compensating by subsidies for these obstacles, and in large measure this removal was the path chosen by both Korea and Singapore. Furthermore, removing the obstacles does not run the risk of attracting countervailing import duties in other countries.

Notes and References

Notes

This chapter is based, with permission, on Aw 1990 and Kim 1990.

1. Nonfactor services as well as merchandise exports are included (World Bank 1987b).

2. Exemptions from indirect taxes and from import tariffs on goods used as inputs into exports are not included in the export subsidies.

3. "Effective" protection attempts to take into account taxes and subsidies on inputs into production processes as well as on outputs.

References

Anderson, Kym, and Yujiro Hayami. 1986. *The Political Economy of Agricultural Protection*. Sydney: Allen and Unwin in association with the Australia-Japan Research Centre, Australian National University.

Aw, Bee-Yan. 1990. "Singapore." In *The Experience of Korea, the Philippines, and Singapore*. Vol. 2 in Liberalizing Foreign Trade, ed. D. Papageorgiou, M. Michaely, and A. M. Choksi. Oxford: Basil Blackwell.

Balassa, Bela, et al. 1982. *Development Strategies in Semi-industrial Economies*. Baltimore: Johns Hopkins University Press for the World Bank.

Hong, Wontack. 1979. *Trade, Distortions and Employment Growth in Korea*. Seoul: Korea Development Institute.

Kim, Kwang Suk. 1990. "Korea." In *The Experience of Korea, the Philippines, and Singapore*. Vol. 2 in Liberalizing Foreign Trade, ed. D. Papageorgiou, M. Michaely, and A. M. Choksi. Oxford: Basil Blackwell.

Krueger, Anne O. 1987. "The Importance of Economic Policy in Development: Contrasts between Korea and Turkey." In Henryk Kierzkowski, ed. *Protection and Competition in International Trade: Essays in Honor of W. M. Corden*. Oxford: Basil Blackwell.

Nam, Chong-Hyun. 1986. Trade Policy and Economic Development in Korea, Washington, D.C.: World Bank, April.

World Bank. 1984. *Korea: Development in a Global Context*. A World Bank Country Study. Washington, D.C.

———. 1987a. *Korea: Managing the Industrial Transition*. Vol. 1, *The Conduct of Industrial Policy*. A World Bank Country Study. Washington, D.C.

———. 1987b. *World Development Report*. New York: Oxford University Press for the World Bank.

The Lessons of Experience: An Overview

This chapter will summarize the major conclusions that tentatively emerge from the World Bank's comparative study of trade-liberalization policies in nineteen countries in the postwar period, discussed in the Introduction. The basic units of observation were liberalization "episodes." An episode is defined as starting with the introduction of some obvious elements of trade liberalization and as ending either when these policies are reversed or when, alternatively, no further clear-cut measures of liberalization are undertaken. Table 10.1 lists the liberalization episodes which have been identified (the time span of each episode is given in parentheses).

The Attributes of Persistent Liberalizers

If we classify the nineteen countries into those which have pursued rather persistently a trade liberalization policy, once started, against those that kept wavering, some systematic differences between the two categories of countries appear.

Among the eight liberalizers, over half are definitely small countries in terms of geographical size. Only one, Indonesia, could probably be classified as large; whereas three others—Chile, New Zealand, and Spain—are roughly medium sized.

The majority of the liberalizing group consists of resource-poor countries, whereas more than half of the nonliberalizers are countries rich in resources. The difference between the two groups is not overwhelming, however.

TABLE 10.1   Episodes of Liberalization, 1950–1984

Latin America			Asia and Pacific			Mediterranean		
Argentina	1	(1967–70)	Indonesia	1	(1950–51)	Greece	1	(1953–55)
Argentina	2	(1970–80)	Indonesia	2	(1966–72)	Greece	2	(1962–82)
Brazil		(1965–73)	Korea	1	(1965–67)	Israel	1	(1952–55)
			Korea	2	(1978–79)	Israel	2	(1962–68)
						Israel	3	(1969–77)
Chile	1	(1956–61)	New Zealand	1	(1951–56)	Portugal	1	(1970–74)
Chile	2	(1974–81)	New Zealand	2	(1962–81)	Portugal	2	(1977–80)
			New Zealand	3	(1982–84)			
Colombia	1	(1964–66)	Pakistan	1	(1959–65)	Spain	1	(1960–66)
Colombia	2	(1968–82)	Pakistan	2	(1972–78)	Spain	2	(1970–74)
						Spain	3	(1977–80)
Peru		(1979–80)	Philippines	1	(1960–65)	Turkey	1	(1970–73)
			Philippines	2	(1970–74)	Turkey	2	(1980–84)
Uruguay		(1974–82)	Singapore		(1968–73)	Yugoslavia		(1965–67)
			Sri Lanka	1	(1968–70)			
			Sri Lanka	2	(1977–79)			

SOURCE: Author.

The combination of these two criteria suggests an even stronger inference: countries which are both small and resource-poor tend to liberalize. Of the six countries characterized by this combination, four (Greece, Israel, Korea, and Singapore) are found among the liberalizers. Of the three countries that are definitely large and rich, on the other hand—Argentina, Brazil, and Indonesia—only the latter belongs among the liberalizers. Of the four that are rich and have middle-sized territories—Colombia, New Zealand, Peru, and the Philippines—only New Zealand has followed a long-term course of liberalization.

Per capita income, an indication (neither well defined nor feasibly measured) of the country's "level of development," does seem to be a relevant factor distinguishing between the two groups of countries. By and large, the liberalizing group consists of countries with a higher per capita income than the nonliberalizers. Thus, relatively richer (on the eve of the potential era of liberalization) countries like Indonesia or Korea are liberalizers. An overlap clearly exists, and opposite cases can be found. Nevertheless, the inference that countries with higher starting income levels are more likely to pursue a course of liberalization than poorer countries does seem to be warranted.

Granted that caution is required by the very tentative nature of any political characterization, it is nevertheless striking that all the eight countries that followed a long-term course of liberalization are found to have had stable political regimes. To put it differently, of the twelve countries with stable political regimes, eight have been liberalizers, and only four have not; whereas all seven countries with unstable regimes manifest an absence of long-term liberalization policy. On the basis of this evidence, it would seem that long-term stability of the political regime is a necessary condition for the long-term pursuance of a trade-liberalization policy. It is not a sufficient condition, yet its existence is likely to result in a long-term course of liberalization.

The long-term performance of the real rate of foreign exchange clearly differentiates liberalizers from nonliberalizers. It is not the direction or extent of the trend change of this variable which matters, however; it is, rather, the absence of violent fluctuations. In other words, liberalizers have tended to be persistent in maintaining a more-or-less given level of the real exchange rate over the long run; whereas nonliberalizers have tended to let this rate suffer from spasms. This difference suggests how important is the predictability of the level of this crucial price as a significant ingredient in a policy that sustains trade liberalization over the long haul.

The liberalizing countries have tended, as a rule, to maintain a significantly smaller budgetary deficit than the nonliberalizers.

Export growth is considerably larger—nearly twice as large—in the liberalizing group of countries than in the other group. Among the nonliberalizers only one country—Yugoslavia—shows a rate of export growth which is above the average (or median) of the group of liberalizers; all the rest are far below it. It may also be noted that in all the liberalizing countries, export growth exceeded—usually by much—the growth of GDP (that is, the share of exports in domestic product has been rising); for the group as a whole, export growth was nearly twice the growth of GDP. For the nonliberalizers, on the other hand, export growth has not generally been this great; and, on average, their export and GDP growth rates were rather similar.

Time Patterns and Sustainability of Liberalization

Strong liberalization attempts tend to be sustained. These are mostly episodes which start with significant, rather than minor and marginal, steps of liberalization. Weak, hesitant liberalization attempts, on the other hand, tend to end up in failure rather than to gather momentum and develop eventually into a major liberalization.

The observations suggest six years as a watershed: if a liberalization attempt survives for that period of time long-term persistence of the policy, or at least its partial survival, appears to be highly likely. A priori, it may be clearly expected that the longer the policy survives, the higher are its chances of being sustained indefinitely; but the specific length of time indicated by the empirical observation—the six-year period—cannot be supported by any presumptive reasoning. One possible hypothesis, which may be very tentatively suggested, is that if a policy lasts that long it must have been carried over from one political environment to another (or it has been applied under a long-term, stable regime); whereas radical policy changes due to transformations of the political regime may be expected to appear within a shorter time.

It appears that an earlier failure, particularly the failure of a serious liberalization attempt, requires that the subsequent attempt at liberalization be strong if it is to have a good chance of success. After a different experience, one of prior success, even a weak program of further liberalization is likely to survive.

A regime of trade restrictions is, in time, self-reinforcing. The longer the regime lasts, the less likely to succeed is any attempt to reverse it, and the more protracted does its life thus become. This, in turn, implies that the initial strength of a liberalization attempt is particularly important for lending it a high probability of survival, in countries with a long history of trade restrictions.

Introduction Circumstances of Liberalization Policies

There appears to be a definite positive relationship between both the strength and the speed of the liberalization policy and the extent to which this policy was introduced under conditions of economic duress.

Liberalization policies implemented under extreme duress are more likely to succeed than those started during "normal" economic performance—although only a minority of the latter, too, have collapsed. It appears least conducive to sustainability to launch a policy at a time when some economic failure is perceived but the failure falls short of a complete economic collapse.

Past experience does not provide any strong evidence that the survival of a liberalization attempt depends in a significant way on any particular motivation for the introduction of the policy—or, in fact, on any specific combination of motivations.

The framework of a multinational commitment, and the desire to share in a multinational agreement, may be a contributing factor to the survival of liberalization once some other, fundamental elements are in operation; in such circumstances, the external commitment may prevent minor and temporary aberrations. When such fundamental components are absent, on the other hand, a multinational framework will not ensure the survival of a liberalization program. The same can be said of policies adopted in response to the urging of outside entities—most often the United States government, the World Bank, or the IMF. These policies are no more likely to survive than liberalizations adopted purely of the countries' own volition. Apparently, again, the timing of liberalizations is influenced by the need to accommodate; but the longer-term course and fate of the liberalization are determined by performances and developments which owe little to the relationships with outside organizations.

Trade Liberalization and Unemployment

The issue of interest is the net impact of liberalization on unemployment. To the extent that a disemployment of factors does not result in any net decline of employment in the overall economy, it simply represents the reallocation of factors, the achievement of which is the major target of liberalization; no short-term costs are then indicated. A net decline of employment, on the other hand, represents a discharge of resource without reassignment to another activity and would thus be a short-term cost to the economy.

A clear-cut general inference is indicated by the data and analyses of the country studies; namely, by and large, liberalization attempts have not resulted in significant transition costs by way of unemployment. In just a few liberalization episodes is there suspicion of a slight negative impact of liberalization on employment: Argentina's two episodes, the Philippines' first episode, and Spain's liberalization episodes. In Chile's second episode, the analysis indicates a substantial impact of liberalization on the structure of employment: a significant decline in manufacturing, matched by an increase in agriculture and nontradables. But no net unemployment should be assigned here, either, to the policy of liberalization.

Since liberalization almost always involves, in a developing economy, reduced protection of manufactures, negative employment consequences should show up first and heaviest in this sector. In fact, a review of the data indicates only a single instance—the aforementioned second episode of Chile—in which employment in manufacturing declined during the liberalization period. This evidence lends support to the general finding that liberalization does not have a negative impact on employment.

It might be argued that this general absence of impact is due to the way liberalization attempts have actually been carried out—specifically, that liberalization has very often produced little change in imports and that many liberalization episodes have been very long and drawn out, so that no transitional costs should have been expected. The series of studies cannot provide a clear-cut answer to the question of what would happen in policy episodes which fell entirely beyond the range of the policies that have actually been practiced. Some clue may be suggested, however, by noting that limiting our observation of past experiences only to strong episodes of liberalization, or even to the narrower group of strong and rapid episodes, would not change our former inference. Chile's second episode was by far the most intense liberalization experience observed, combining the most comprehensive scope with a short span of time for completion; and, we have seen, this liberalization created no net unemployment. In general, the data suggest no relationship between the intensity of liberalization and its impact on unemployment.

The fate of liberalization has rarely been determined, or even significantly affected, by unemployment. Only two instances are mentioned in which some such relationship exists; and even there, it is in a weak form. In his study of Yugoslavia's liberalization episode (1965–1967), Havrylyshyn (1990) concludes that the policy reversal in 1968 may to a large extent be assigned to the public's perception that the liberalization led to a slowdown of growth (rather than unemployment). In Israel, a recession in 1965 and 1966, in the middle of the country's second liberalization episode (1962–1968), led in the judgment of Halevi and Baruh (1990) to a temporary abstention from (rather than reversal of) further expansion of liberalization. The collective evidence of the findings in the country studies suggests, in general, almost no impact of unemployment on the course of a liberalization policy. Even if we ignore the inferences drawn by the authors of the country studies, however, and assume that a causal relationship can be found in a temporal sequence, it appears that only in very few episodes could the reversal of liberalization be potentially assigned to unemployment. Thus, in addition to our earlier inference that liberalization has not, by and large, led to significant short-term unemployment, we reach a similar conclusion about the reverse causality—namely, by and large, when unemployment has emerged, for whatever reason, it has not been significant in determining the fate of liberalization policy.

Trade Liberalization and the Balance of Payments

No relationship can be established between the level of foreign-exchange reserves on the eve of liberalization and the likelihood that the policy will eventually succeed, in terms of survival. This is a significant finding: neither a favorable nor a deteriorating balance of payments (judged by the level of foreign-exchange reserves or changes therein) at the start of liberalization appears, from past experience, to be a precondition for or a guarantor of the longer-term survival of the policy. Nor does a prior (to the implementation of liberalization) increasing trend of exports tend to increase the likelihood that a liberalization attempt will survive.

In the large majority of the instances in which a favorable change in the trend movement of foreign-exchange reserves is evident, a favorable change in export performance also appears to have taken place; most often, this change is a reversal from an export contraction to an expansion. A very strong association thus seems to exist between the improvement of export performance and the overall improvement of the country's balance of payments.

The impact of liberalization measures on the balance of payments and on its elements seems not to have been a factor of any general importance in determining the survival of trade-liberalization experiences.

A strong association is established between failures of liberalization attempts and declining foreign-exchange reserves toward the *end* of liberalization episodes and between policy survival and a favorable balance-of-payments performance. The data do suggest causality and dependence.

Similarly, the survival of liberalization attempts tends strongly to be related to a favorable export performance, whereas the collapse of liberalization is overwhelmingly connected with a dismal export performance.

No systematic connection, however, seems to exist between the adoption of export-promotion measures, as a component of the trade-liberalization package, and the sustainability of a liberalization policy. Nor does the introduction of an export-promotion policy before import liberalization seem to add materially to the likelihood that trade reform will survive.

The Relaxation of Quantitative Restrictions (QRs)

In no single case in which QRs were prevalent has a liberalization process started with a reduction of tariff levels and left QRs untouched. Obviously, in a system in which QRs were effective, tariff reductions would mean only, if anything, a reduction in tariff collection. An irrational policy of this nature has never been observed in the countries and periods studied in the World Bank project.

In the many instances in which the liberalization process started with a relaxation of QRs, this relaxation has been reversed (although, it should be noted, less frequently than in other episodes); has not been followed at all by tariff reductions yet has persisted, on its own, with no reversal; has been followed by tariff reductions after a long while; and, on two occasions, has been followed by tariff reductions after only a short interval. Starting with only a relaxation of QRs (whether or not compensated by tariff increases) and then proceeding to tariff reductions within a relatively short time has thus been the exception.

The nineteen liberalization episodes which were classified as strong—roughly half of all liberalization experiences—divide about equally into episodes in which a major relaxation of QRs was undertaken, and others. In the first category, sustainability has been practically universal; in the second, it has been the exception. Thus, all the previously noted positive relationship between intensity of liberalizations and their sustainability is due to the powerful association of the two in QR-relaxing episodes. This collective experience strongly suggests that, starting with a restrictive regime in which QRs are of the essence, a liberalization policy is likely to survive if it starts with a stage of radical relaxation of QRs, and it is likely to fail without it.

In general, undertaking a serious attempt to relax a regime of QRs may not be motivated overwhelmingly either by a situation of duress or, to the contrary, by a particularly favorable set of economic circumstances. It should be noted, though, that most episodes preceded by a perception of total economic collapse do include an element of major relaxation of QRs.

Episodes with major relaxation of QRs form the most radical liberalizations; hence, transitory adjustment costs of these episodes might have been expected to be particularly high. In fact, these episodes demonstrate a remarkable increase of economic growth in the years immediately following the liberalization. This lesson is of great significance. Undoubtedly, this growth also helps to explain the universal sustainability of liberalization policies launched in this form.

QRs may be administered through, alternatively, positive or negative lists. The negative list provides the benefit of leaving future, yet-undeveloped activities free of restrictions. Perhaps more important, though its impact is not easily measurable, is the change in the economic regime's nature that the shift from a positive to a negative list indicates: in the former scheme, everything is presumed to be prohibited unless specifically allowed, whereas in the latter the reverse is true. A still further, more tangible advantage of a negative list is that its existence makes the planning (and announcement) of future relaxation of controls more feasible, since the modification in the list of restrictions explicitly reflects policy changes.

The Role of the Real Exchange Rate in Trade Liberalization

A strong qualitative relationship is established between the behavior of the real exchange rate when liberalization is launched and the fate of the policy: the liberalization is likely to be sustained when the exchange rate increases and to collapse when it falls. An increase of the real rate appears to be almost a necessary condition for at least a partial survival of a liberalization policy.

A somewhat weaker, but still obvious relationship exists between the sustainability of liberalizations and the performance of the exchange rate throughout the lifetime of the episode. In the overwhelming majority of the instances in which the exchange rate increased during the liberalization episode the episode was fully or partially sustained. When no trend change of the exchange rate was evident, the record of sustainability is mixed. Whenever the real exchange rate falls during an episode, liberalization tends to collapse.

A clear-cut relationship exists also between the performance of the real exchange rate toward the close of the liberalization episode and the fate of the episode. An increase of the exchange rate is associated with survival of liberalization; and a fall of the rate, with its collapse.

It appears that all three of these periodical indicators—the movement of the real exchange rate at the beginning of a liberalization episode, during the episode, and at its close—are clearly related to the sustainability of liberalization. A rise in the exchange rate, in all these periodical dimensions, tends to be associated with the survival of a liberalization policy.

A nominal devaluation seems to be almost a necessary condition for a real devaluation: of sixteen liberalization episodes in which the real rate increased, in fourteen a nominal devaluation was also present. Conversely, in the clear majority of episodes in which the nominal rate increased, so did the real rate. The number of exceptions, however, is large enough to preclude a statement that a nominal devaluation is also, empirically speaking, a sufficient condition for a real one. An initial nominal devaluation, if substantial, is an important contributory element in achieving a persistent increase in the real exchange rate.

Where all the policy elements were right—where a nominal devaluation was accompanied by tight fiscal and monetary policies—an increased real exchange rate normally followed. It is not easy to tell which of the two demand-policy requirements—tight fiscal policy or tight monetary policy—is more crucial for realizing an increase in the real exchange rate. Although neither seems to be a necessary condition in the same sense that a nominal devaluation is, both are important—and, certainly, if neither is present there is likely to be no increase in the real exchange rate.

Note and References

Note

This chapter is based on Michaely, Papageorgiou, and Choksi 1990.

References

Halevi, Nadav, and Joseph Baruh. 1990. "Israel." In *The Experience of Israel and Yugoslavia*. Vol. 3 in Liberalizing Foreign Trade, ed. D. Papageorgiou, M. Michaely, and A. M. Choksi. Oxford: Basil Blackwell.

Havrylyshyn, Oli. 1990. "Yugoslavia." In *The Experience of Israel and Yugoslavia*. Vol. 3 in Liberalizing Foreign Trade, ed. D. Papageorgiou, M. Michaely, and A. M. Choksi. Oxford: Basil Blackwell.

Michaely, Michael, Demetris Papageorgiou, and Armeane M. Choksi. 1990. *Lessons of Experience in the Developing World*. Vol. 7 in Liberalizing Foreign Trade, ed. D. Papageorgiou, M. Michaely, and A. M. Choksi. Oxford: Basil Blackwell.

About the Contributors

GEOFFREY SHEPHERD is an economist in the Brazil Department of the World Bank. Before joining the Brazil Department he helped prepare the Bank's *World Development Report 1987*. Shepherd received his D.Phil. from the University of Sussex, where he was also deputy director of the Sussex European Research Centre and a senior fellow at the Science Policy Research Unit.

CARLOS GERALDO LANGONI is director of the Center for the World Economy of the Getúlio Vargas Foundation in Rio de Janeiro. He is also president of Projeta Consultoria Financeira S/C Ltda. (associated with N. M. Rothschild) and a consultant on strategic planning, economic and financial trends, and debt-equity conversions to a number of Brazilian companies. He has been director of the Graduate School of Economics of the Getúlio Vargas Foundation and governor of the central bank of Brazil. He is the author of *The Development Crisis: Blueprint for Change*, published by ICS Press in 1987.

DOMINGO F. CAVALLO is the minister of foreign affairs in Argentina. He is also a member of the National House of Deputies, a consultant to IEERAL of the Fundación Mediterranea, and a member of the *World Bank Research Observer* editorial board. Cavallo earned a doctorate in economic sciences from the National University of Córdoba and a Ph.D. from Harvard University and has taught at the National University of Córdoba and the Catholic University of Córdoba. He is president of the Standing Committee of the Latin American Chapter of the Econometric

Society and has published books, monographs, and articles on fiscal problems, exchange rates, trade, agriculture, and other areas of economic policy.

DONALD COES is professor of international management at the Anderson School of Management and associate director of the Latin American Institute, University of New Mexico. He has also been a senior economist at the Centro de Estudos do Comércio Exterior in Rio de Janeiro and an international economist at the U.S. Agency for International Development. A graduate of Harvard University, he received his Ph.D. from Princeton University. He is a member of several professional organizations and is the author of many publications in Europe, the United States, and Latin America on international trade and development.

GUILLERMO DE LA DEHESA is currently chief executive of the Banco Pastor in Madrid, European adviser to Goldman Sachs, a member of the Group of Thirty, and a member of the Centre for Economic Policy Research (CEPR) in London. He has served in a number of government departments and has been secretary of state for economy in the Ministry of Economy and Finance. He holds degrees in both law and economics from Madrid University and has represented his country in several international organizations, assemblies, and committees. His published works include papers in economic reviews, other articles, and lectures.

PAULO TARSO FLECHA DE LIMA is Brazil's ambassador to the United Kingdom. During a long diplomatic career, he has held posts in Rome, Montevideo, and New York; further, in the top diplomatic position of secretary-general of external relations for Brazil, he on several occasions served as acting minister of external relations. Before entering the foreign service, Flecha de Lima earned a degree from the Law School of the University of Brazil.

DOMINIQUE HACHETTE is a professor of economics at Catholic University, Santiago, Chile. First educated in Chile and France, he obtained his Ph.D. from the University of Chicago, where he specialized in international trade and development. During his career, he has also been a visiting professor at the Universidad de Nueva León, Mexico, and the Universidad de los Andes, Colombia; head of statistics in a private business in Chile; and an economist with the central bank of Chile. He has published widely on issues of trade reform, balance of payments, and other international trade issues.

OLI HAVRYLYSHYN is currently working in the Country Economics Department of the World Bank, on leave from the Department of Economics at George Washington University. After receiving his Ph.D. in economics from the Massachusetts Institute of Technology, he taught at Queen's University, Canada. He has also been a visiting scholar at the Université Libre in Brussels and at the Graduate Institute of International Studies in Geneva. Havrylyshyn has lived and worked extensively in the third world and Europe and has been associated with the World Bank, the Canadian International Development Agency, and other international institutions. He has published widely on international trade and third world development.

MICHAEL MICHAELY, who received his Ph.D. from Johns Hopkins University, is the lead economist in the Brazil Department of the World Bank. He has been the Aron and Michael Chilewich Professor of International Trade and dean of the faculty of social sciences at the Hebrew University of Jerusalem. He has also been president of the Israel Economic Association and a visiting professor or visiting scholar at universities in Australia, Sweden, and the United States. He is the author of books and articles on various aspects of international economics, including exchange-rate policies, macroeconomic adjustment, and the structure of world trade.

DEMETRIS PAPAGEORGIOU is currently the chief of the Country Operations Division in the Brazil Department of the World Bank. He has been a senior economist in the Country Policy Department and an economist in the Industry Division of the Development Economics Department of the World Bank. He attended graduate school at Duke University, where he taught trade and applied price theory. He is coeditor, with Armeane M. Choksi, of *Economic Liberalization in Developing Countries* and has written extensively on issues of industrial and trade policy.

RICHARD H. SNAPE was educated at the University of Melbourne, Australia, and the London School of Economics. He is currently chairman of the Department of Economics at Monash University, Melbourne. He has been editor of the *World Bank Economic Review* and the *World Bank Research Observer* and has held a number of advisory positions with the government of Australia. He was also editor of the *Economic Record* for a number of years and has taught at the Institute of International Economics in Stockholm. Snape has published several books on international trade policy.

Index

Yugoslavia, 94
Price mechanism
Argentina, 28
Chile, 43, 48, 52
Greece, 61–62, 66
Yugoslavia, 99
Privatization, Chile, 44
Protection levels
Argentina, 108
Brazil, 15
Chile, 41, 45, 48–49
Greece, 63
Korea (South), 105–6, 108
Spain, 78
Yugoslavia, 99

Quantitative restrictions (QRs)
effect of relaxation of, 8, 123–25
Argentina, 30
Chile, 50–51
Greece, 61
Korea (South), 105–6
Spain, 80, 82–83

Real exchange rate (RER)
in trade liberalization, 125–26
Argentina
appreciation and depreciation of, 36
effect of fall of, 35–36
Chile, 44, 48, 50
Recession, Chile, 43, 45
Recession, world, 48
Remittances, Yugoslavia, 92
RER. *See* Real exchange rate (RER)
RERM. *See* Multilateral exchange rate (RERM), Argentina

Savings, Spain, 84
Single European Act: EEC, 81
Special Program of Fiscal Incentives for Exporters (BEFIEX): Brazil, 18
Spending, government
Chile, 43
Greece, 66
Singapore, 113–14
State-owned enterprises, Chile, 44

Subsidies
Argentina, 31–32, 38
Greece, 68–69
Korea (South), 108, 114
Singapore, 114
Spain, 83–84
Yugoslavia, 92, 95, 98–100

Tariff Policy Council (CPA): Brazil, 17
Tariffs
timing in trade reform for, 8
Argentina, 30, 31–32
Brazil, 12–13, 16–17
Chile
increase in, 49
reduction in, 41–43, 45, 49
Korea (South), 105–6
Spain, 82
reduction in, 78, 80, 81
reform for, 77
Yugoslavia, 98–99
Tax policy
Argentina, 30, 31, 108
Brazil, 16
Chile, 43
Singapore, 108
Spain, 83
Tourism, Yugoslavia, 92
Trade-liberalization episodes, 117
Trade-liberalization index, Korea (South), 104
Trade policy
characteristics of liberalization of, 7–8, 117, 119–21
benefits of liberalization of, 96
sustainability and timing of liberalization of, 119–20
Argentina, 31–32
Brazil
coordination of exchange-rate policy and, 24
effect of proposed deregulation of, 13–14
parameters for deregulation in, 12–13
reforms of, 1964–1974, 15
requirements for reform of, 3–4

A seven-volume series detailing the results of the
World Bank project on the timing and sequencing of
trade liberalization

Liberalizing Foreign Trade
Edited by
Demetris Papageorgiou, Michael Michaely,
and Armeane M. Choksi
Directors of the Project

Volume 1 *The Experience of Argentina, Chile, and Uruguay*   cloth $75.00
0-631-16666-1

Volume 2 *The Experience of Korea, the Philippines, and*   cloth $75.00
Singapore   0-631-16667-X

Volume 3 *The Experience of Israel and Yugoslavia*   cloth $75.00
0-631-16668-8

Volume 4 *The Experience of Brazil, Colombia, and Peru*   cloth $75.00
0-631-16669-6

Volume 5 *The Experience of Indonesia, Pakistan, and*   cloth $75.00
Sri Lanka   0-631-16671-8

Volume 6 *The Experience of Spain, New Zealand, and*   cloth $75.00
Turkey   0-631-16672-6

Volume 7 *Lessons of Experience in the Developing World*   cloth $75.00
0-631-16673-4

7-Volume Set   cloth $525.00
0-631-17595-4

An essential reference and research source
Available from
Basil Blackwell, Inc.
Three Cambridge Center, Cambridge, MA 02142
Telephone: (617) 225-0430 / FAX: (617) 494-1437

ICEG Academic Advisory Board